AUSTRALIAN   SEA   SERPENTS

Malcolm Smith

Australian Sea Serpents

Independently published 2020

1. Sea Serpents   2. Cryptozoology   3. Australia

4. Folklore   5. Marine Mysteries

ISBN: 9798615873454

Front cover: Captain Millar's initial sketch of the *Dimboola* sea serpent of 1913

Contents

INTRODUCTION

Sea Serpents! Aren't they the sort of things medieval map makers used to place in the distant oceans? Not really. It is true that cartographers used to decorate the blank spaces on the their maps (not necessarily seas) with imaginative monsters (not necessarily serpentine). However, they were never intended as anything other than whimsical illustrations. The legend of the sea serpent, if you can call it that, did not commence until the sixteenth century, when Scandinavian traditions about the creature were introduced to the outside world. Its heyday was the nineteenth century, when both the press and the scientific establishment took it seriously. This was the period of a great expansion of maritime trade, with sailing vessels moved silently across the oceans, frequently driven out of the normal sea lanes. Noisy steamships confined to narrow lanes make it more difficult to notice rare sea monsters, but nevertheless, the tradition continued into the first half of the twentieth century, as we shall see.

Altogether, there have been three omnibus tomes designed to analyse the data on this mystery. *The Great Sea-Serpent* (1892) by Antoon C. Oudemans was followed in 1930 by *The Case for the Sea-Serpent* by R. T. Gould. However, the most comprehensive, almost encyclopaedic tome, admittedly now half a century old, is *In the Wake of the Sea-Serpents* by Bernard Heuvelmans.[1] This remarkable zoologist catalogued 587 reports worldwide from before 1639 up to 1966. After dismissing all apparent or probable hoaxes and mistakes, plus those too vague or questionable to be considered, he was still left with 349 reports which ought to be taken seriously - about one a year.

Not only that, but it was apparent, surprisingly enough, that there exists more than one type of sea serpent. Not everyone would agree with the nine categories he came up with, but there are a couple which must be mentioned, because similar types turn up in Australian shores. One of them is of similar size to a whale, but is elongated, with a short neck and a row of humps along the body. It also swims by means of vertically undulations, which demonstrates that it must be a mammal. Zoology 101 teaches us that, whereas fish and reptiles move by flexing their bodies horizontally, and their tail fin, if they have one, is vertical, mammalian bodies flex vertically when moving, and any tail fluke is horizontal. And there were prehistoric whales which were serpentine in shape.

The second type is the "long-necked" sea serpent, characterized by a long neck like a periscope protruding from the water, often to be followed by a thick body with one, two, or three humps. In some, the eyes are very small, even invisible, while in others they are very large. For this reason, Heuvelmans considers them two different species, but I shall not push the issue here. What they might be is a mystery, but for reasons I shall provide later, I am prepared to rule out the two most popular theories. However superficially they may resemble them, they are not those prehistoric reptiles from the age of dinosaurs known as plesiosaurs. Nor, with all due respect to Heuvelmans and his two predecessors, do I believe they are some sort of long-necked seal.

Also, to make matters more interesting, some of the visitors to our shores are weird even by sea serpent standards.

In 1996 I included a lengthy chapter on sea serpents in my book, *Bunyips and Bigfoots*. Since then, several people have approached me with reports of their own. However, the major innovation has been the development of Trove[2], the National Library of Australia's program of digitalising nearly every Australian newspaper up to the mid-1950s, which has allowed me to research stories previously known only from paraphrases in secondary sources, not to mention discovering cases not previously known. In fact, more than half the material here is new ie never published in book form before, and much of the rest has been amplified.

At this point, I should explain that the reports nearly all cite Imperial measures (yards, feet, and inches) with which many of my younger readers, brought up on metrics, will be unfamiliar. However, since I do not wish to mess with the crude data, and since I also expect the book to be read in America, I have chosen not to replace the original estimates of size, but to include the metric equivalents as well. No attempt has been made to provide more accuracy than was present in the original. For example, a yard is approximately 90 cm, but considering the normal inaccuracies in estimates of distance, a yard is as good as a metre.

Bear in mind, too, that without some frame of reference, estimates of distance and size at sea are of questionable validity. Furthermore, a witness under the influence of fear or astonishment is liable to exaggerate. Thus, when a witness states that the sea serpent was 200 yards from shore and 80 feet [24 metres] long, all that really can be said is: it was really big, and quite some distance away.

There were two things I did discover, however, when trawling through Trove. The first is that the same story tended to get picked up by various newspapers all over the country, often after lapses of several days, or even weeks. I have therefore chosen to cite what appears to be the earliest and/or most detailed reference, but you can certainly find a lot of others, if you are that way inclined.

The second is that the journalists reported nothing except what the witness(es) volunteered, and failed to request any further information. This reflects badly on the journalists. If you work for a newspaper, and you receive a report of a sea serpent - or a yowie, flying saucer, ghost, or such - then either you are on to something big or you are on to something stupid. It behoves you to dig a little deeper and obtain information which may assist later investigators. (I shall discuss this in more detail later.)

But at least they took it seriously - which is more than what tends to happen today. Later in the book you will hear of a man who, in 1995, slipped the report of his sighting under the door of the local newspaper anonymously, because he did not wish adverse publicity. The following year I was commissioned by Yorkshire Television to locate witnesses to appear on one of their documentaries. That I succeeded was in spite of the fact that nobody of any standing in the community wanted to get involved. In fact, one witness, who was now a radio compère, offered to interview *me*, but I was given strict instructions not to mention his own experience.

It makes you wonder how many experiences are "out there" and never see the light of day.

ACKNOWLEDGEMENTS

I often wonder if anyone reads the long lists of acknowledgements typical of most non-fiction. Still, I might be surprised. I once ran my eyes down one list and was surprised to discover my own name herein. Then I vaguely remembered corresponding with the author years before on a very minor issue. So, as a matter of politeness, not to mention genuine gratitude, I would like to thank the following:

Firstly, there is Paul Cropper, who discovered many of these old reports, and with whom I collaborated in a paper in the now defunct journal, *Cryptozoology*. Then there is the late Dr Bernard Heuvelmans himself, Dr Jeff Johnson, Peter Chapple, and Gerald L. Wood.

Special acknowledgement is also due to those witnesses and others who were kind enough to respond to my enquiries, and whose accounts will be found in the relevant chapters:

Robyn Beecham, Neil Blyth, Carol Borck, John Gardenne, J. Richard Greenwell, Dan Guillespie, Meg Lloyd, Kevin Maley, Simon Moir, Norman Robertson, Nigel Tutt, Simon Townsend, and Joy Zeller.

1. Two Big Fish

The sea, if you come to think of it, is an alien world for us. We normally view it only from the surface, and on the rare occasions when we go deeper, our view is limited to very short distances. True, we catch a lot of its inhabitants. But ask yourself how many land animals would escape notice if we collected them by merely casting baited lines into the forest, or swept the grasslands with nets. So it is not at all outrageous to consider that relatively uncommon large species whose anatomy and habits prevent them from falling foul of our lines and nets, and which are able to slither away if they run aground, might still exist undetected in our oceans.

Thus, in 1976, a shark got entangled in a sea anchor of an American ship off Hawaii, and was discovered to be completely new to science. Labeled *Megachasma pelagios*, or megamouth shark, it turned out to be a filter-feeding fish reaching 5.2 metres, or 17 feet in length. In the four decades since its discovery, 63 specimens have been sighted or taken - which makes one wonder where it was before then.

So now, since sea serpents still possess an aura of the fantastic, we shall dip our toes into the shallow end of this sea of mystery by having a look at what might be unknown big fish in our adjacent waters.

Let's start off with *Jaws*, the great white shark, *Carcharodon carcharias*, one of the largest flesh-eating sharks. There are much larger sharks, but they are harmless plankton feeders. How large? It is always a bit artificial to record the maximum size of any species. After all, the "maximum size" of human beings is 272 cm [8 ft 11 in], recorded for the unfortunate Robert Wadlow (1918 - 1940) who was a victim of pituitary giantism. However, we know from experience that very few people pass 193 cm [6ft 4 in], even among tall races, and 203 cm [6ft 8 in] is probably the non-pathological maximum.

Likewise, freakishly large specimens occur in all species. Also, most "cold blooded" animals never actually stop growing, but continue increasing in size, albeit slowly, throughout life. Thus, every individual measured will be smaller than the maximum. For the great white shark, therefore, expect a really big specimen to measure 5.2 metres [17 feet], with 6.1 metres [20 feet] being the "normal" maximum, but it is possible some a little longer have put in an appearance.

However, between 23 and 2½ million years ago there existed a real monster known as the megalodon ("big tooth") shark, or *Carcharocles megalodon*. As shark skeletons consist of cartilage rather than bone, they do not fossilise well. Therefore, apart from a few vertebrae, the only fossils we have of this nightmare are its teeth, which make estimating its length somewhat difficult. The most reasonable estimate is 18.3 metres, or 60 feet: a shark the size of whales, which preyed on whales!

It is frightening to think, therefore, that there are claims that it may still be alive today. In my earlier book I rather uncritically repeated the alleged evidence. However, Ben S. Roesch, who is both a shark expert and a cryptozoologist, or student of mystery animals, has published an article effectively demolishing these claims[3]. He points out that *C. megalodon* would have haunted shallow seas, where it would hardly have gone unnoticed, and that the alleged sightings are either undocumented, or more easily explainable as whale sharks, which are much larger than great whites, but eat only plankton.

Nevertheless, there was one report which he could not dispose of in such a manner, but which he considered too fantastic to be true. It was fantastic, but it deserves to be mentioned to allow you to make up your own mind. It occurred at Broughton Island, 14 km northeast of Port Stephens, NSW in 1918, and was recorded by David Stead in his posthumous book, *Sharks and Rays of Australian Seas*[4]. Stead was a fisheries expert who was frequently approached by the press when "sea serpents" were reported, as we shall see later.

> In the year 1918 I recorded the sensation that had been caused among the "outside" crayfish men at Port Stephens, when, for several days, they refused to go to sea to their regular fishing

grounds in the vicinity of Broughton Island. The men had been at work on the fishing grounds - which lie in deep water - when an immense shark of almost unbelievable proportions put in an appearance, lifting pot after pot containing many crayfish, and taking, as the men said, "pots, mooring lines and all". These crayfish pots, it should be mentioned were about 3 feet 6 inches [107 cm] in diameter and frequently contained from two to three dozen good-sized crayfish each weighing several pounds. The men were all unanimous that this shark was something the like of which they had never dreamed of. In company with the local Fisheries Inspector I questioned many of the men very closely and they all agreed as to the gigantic stature of the beast. But the lengths they gave were, on the whole, absurd. I mention them, however, as an indication of the state of mind which this unusual giant had thrown them into. And bear in mind that these were men who were used to the sea and all sorts of weather, and all sorts of sharks as well. One of the crew said the shark was "three hundred feet [90 m] long at least"! Others said it was as long as the wharf on which we stood - about 115 feet [35 m]! They affirmed that the water "boiled" over a large space when the fish swam past. They were all familiar with whales, which they had often seen passing at sea, but this was a vast shark. They had seen its terrible head which was "at least as long as the roof on the wharf at Nelson's Bay." Impossible, of course! But these were prosaic and rather stolid men, not given to 'fish stories' nor even to talking about their catches. Further, they knew that the person they were talking to (myself) had had all the fish stories years before! One of the things that impressed me was that they all agreed as to the ghostly whitish colour of the vast fish. The local Fisheries Inspector of the time, Mr Paton, agreed with me that it must have been something really gigantic to put their experienced men into such a state of fear and panic.

I have since located the original newspaper accounts of the incident[5], the earliest of which were on 30 January. The source was David Stead himself, who was the Director of the State Trawling Industry. He had asked the fishermen whether they had lost any lobster pots during the recent storm, and then the story came out. The fishermen were apparently Greek, and their amusing variety of

English was included. One interesting snippet was that one of the launches had had to be beached for repairs, because the shark had bitten a piece out of it!

As the event took place at sea rather than in fresh water, I'm assuming that the "crayfish" was *Jasus edwardsii*, known as both the southern rock lobster and the sea crayfish, adults of which range from 350 g to 5 kg. It appears it was the sheer ferocity of the attack which put the fear of hell into the fishermen, kept them from their work for several days, and caused them to grossly over-estimate the size of animal. Just the same, if we assume the average pot contained two dozen individuals weighing an average of a kilogram ("several pounds"), then we are talking about 24 kg per pot. That's a lot of meat to consume if several pots were taken, and indicates that something really huge was responsible. Roesch was critical of the "ghostly whitish colour" of the fish, because the upper parts of the great white are really greyish, and he expected the megalodon shark to have possessed similar counter-shading. On the other hand, Gerald L. Wood, of the *Guinness Book of Records*, was impressed by the reported oversized head, and suggested it might have been an albino sperm whale similar to the fictitious Moby Dick[6]. After all, a completely white sperm whale killed off Peru in 1951 measured 55 feet [16.7 m]. That identification would appear to explain the head and the size, but the ferocity of the attack is more consistent with the feeding frenzy of a shark rather than a sperm whale, which possesses teeth only in the lower jaw, and whose jaw can only move vertically, not sideways.

So, basically, what attacked the crayfish pots in 1918 must remain a mystery.

The second incident took place in the winter of 1994 or 1995 at the beach at Wurtulla, a seaside suburb of Caloundra, Queensland at approximately 28° 48' S, 153° 15' E. Within a period of four days in December 1996 I interviewed by telephone two of the four witnesses, Simon Moir and John Gardenne[7].

Four men who were sharing a house were playing cricket on the beach about 2 p.m. when it occurred. Visibility was good, and the sea choppy, but not very rough, the waves being about one or two feet high (say half a metre). Suddenly, they saw a large fish ploughing through the water about 20 or 30 yards away (according to Moir) or 100 yards out (according to Gardene). It did not display any undulations, either vertical or horizontal. As a diver, Moir was familiar with sharks and rays, and estimated the order of magnitude of its size as similar to that of a five metre grey nurse shark. They could not see the head, but the body was brown in colour. At one point it rolled, and they could see its white underside. The body was broad, like a shark, not narrow and deep like an ordinary rayed fish. Close to shore the beach drops off sharply, and Moir suspected that it had turned back when it arrived at the shallows. The last they saw of it was outside of the breakers.

Both witnesses agreed that its most salient feature was its unusual dorsal fin in the middle, or mid-front of its body. Although not pointed like a shark's, it towered above the waves, being about three or four feet (say a metre) high, and I gained the impression that its length at the base was similar to its height. It was like a fan, brown with a series of white rays, and leaning to the side. At first Moir thought it had been harpooned, with some spikes sticking out of it, but then he realised the spikes were natural. Gardene, in contrast, likened it more to an upside down cow's utter, with the rays out of alignment, but on being questioned, he admitted that it was two-dimensional, like a fin, not three dimensional, like a conning tower. Moir concurred.

What was it? The largest fish are elasmobranchs ie sharks and rays, but this was obviously a teleost, or ray-finned fish. Not being a fish expert, I telephoned Dr Jeff Johnson, the resident ichthyologist at the Queensland Museum. He was unable to identify it either.

How did I learn about this? I was on talk back radio promoting my new book, *Bunyips and Bigfoots*, when Mr Moir called it to tell his story. If I hadn't been on the station that day, or he had not been listening, this report would never have come to light. So how many others are "out there"?

2. The Early Years

At the beginning, while searching through the newspapers of the 1850s and 1860s I was constantly coming across references to a prominent clipper called the *Sea Serpent*. Regrettably, its crew never encountered its namesake, so I was never able to find the headline: "SEA SERPENT SEES SEA SERPENT", but the crews of quite a few other ships did. So let us now have a look at some real, honest-to-goodness sea serpent stories - and to keep track of them, we shall number them.

[1] In 1854 a Danish brig which may have been called the *Jobn* (the word was hard to read) under Captain R. Aschlund, was sailing between Melbourne and Batavia, which is now the Indonesian capital of Jakarta. Several hundred kilometres west of Australia, close to the latitude of Shark Bay, it had the following experience, as described in its log[8]:

'On Sunday, the 8th of January being in S. lat, 24° 30', and E. long. 105° 50', with fine weather and a S. and S.S.W. breeze, we saw in the afternoon, at about half past 5 o'clock, going at about 3½ knots an hour [6½ kph], a large sea-snake, the length of which, according to our calculation, was about 50 feet [15 m], the head about 4 feet [1.2 m], and the body, in the thickest part; in circumference [did he mean 'diameter'?], 4 feet. It swam at a distance of 2 feet [60 cm] from the brig, at a depth of 6 feet [1.8 m] beneath the surface of the water.'

[2] The first record in actual Australian waters did not come to light until 36 to 37 years had passed. In late 1889. the *London Evening Standard* had published an article about sea monsters, which inspired a Mr. Francis Jones to approach the *Evening News* of Sydney with the following story[9].

This morning we are informed by Mr. Francis Jones, newsagent, of North Shore, that in going from Sydney to Rockhampton during the Port Curtis rush in 1862 and 1863 he was a passenger by the steamer City of Sydney. When off Keppel Bay, owing to an accident, she was put at half speed, and while thus going slowly a monster of the deep was seen close to the ship. It was at least 40ft [12 metres] long, in shape like a snake, and very pretty, being striped like some species of Australian snake. There were from 60 to 70 passengers on board, most, if not all of whom in addition to the crew, saw the Australian sea serpent. A good view was obtained owing to his snakeship for some time taking the same course as the steamer.

Keppel Bay is situated at the mouth of the Fitzroy River, near Rockhampton. The sighting is peculiar. As we shall see, sea serpents are very rarely described as striped. Genuine sea snakes do exist, and the greatest number of species do occur in Australian waters. However, the vast majority are less than a metre in length. To be sure, some outsize specimens of the banded sea krait, *Laticauda colubrina* have been known to attain 2.75 metres, and the species is a vivid blue with black bands, all the better to advertise its deadly venom. Nevertheless, the vast majority are only half that length. Also, although a vagrant individual might theoretically reach Keppel Bay, its range is normally much farther away, in southeast Asia and Melanesia. Furthermore, even allowing for exaggeration, what Mr. Jones saw was much too big, as well as being in the wrong area.

[3] The next one was not near Australia proper, but in the waters of its territory, Norfolk Island. To be precise, close to Nepean Island, a small islet just south of Norfolk Island. In this case, the witness was John Adams, the grandson of one of the *Bounty* mutineers, for the descendants of the mutineers had been transferred from their now over-populated home of Pitcairn Island to Norfolk Island after the closure of the convict settlement. And thereby hangs a tale.

Hollywood never made a sequel to *Mutiny on the 'Bounty'*, but six of the mutineers, along with an equal number of Polynesian men, and some Tahitian women, some of whom had been kidnapped, settled on Pitcairn Island. Then followed a sordid story of racial war, lust, drunkenness, and murder, which left only a single adult male alive: John Adams. Now at the end of his tether, Adams started reading the only two books salvaged from the *Bounty*: the Prayer Book and the Bible. Need I say more? What normally happens when a person at the end of his tether comes face to face with the word of God? Within a generation, Pitcairn Island, and later Norfolk Island, had become famous as Christian utopias in the South Seas[10]. So when Captain Marcus Lowther, R.N., referred to Adams' grandson as "a man incapable of telling an untruth"[11], he was probably describing most of the islanders at the time.

1877 was a year of many published sea serpent sightings, so John Adams decided to write to the Literary and Philosophical Society of Liverpool to tell them what he encountered seven years before.[12]

On the 15th October, 1870, wind S.E. and light, our boat being a mile off Nepean Island, and on the port tack, our look-out reported a calf (as the young whale is called) about a mile and a half [2½ km] distant on the lee bow. We accordingly kept off, and when about a hundred yards from the supposed calf, he said - 'I cannot make out what it is; I have not seen a spout yet; but there is an animal of some sort, for his back is out of the water, and there is a wash there all the time.' 'Very well,' was the answer; 'Keep a sharp look out.' On we went till within a few yards of the object, when the look-out exclaimed - 'Look! it is a Sea Serpent!' And look we did. The boat shot within a yard of it, and there it was, a veritable Sea Serpent . . . When first seen, I suppose it must have been asleep, for its head was lying flat on the surface of the sea, and its body coiled up. The tail of the monster I saw plainly, hanging some three or four fathoms [5½ to 7 metres] below the surface. When we came near it, the beast, if I may call it so, raised its head out of the water, looked at us, then slowly straightening himself, he very leisurely moved off. I cannot tell you with any certainty the length of it, for it was not lying with its whole length on the surface, but, as nearly as I could judge, it must have been thirty or forty feet [9 to 12 m]. It was of a reddish colour, and about a foot or eighteen inches [30 to 45 cm] in diameter. We have been about the Island in boats almost every day when the weather's fine for nearly eighteen years, and have never seen anything like it before or since then.

This is so very strange. The description fits a true snake rather than an eel. A vagrant individual of the banded sea snake might conceivably arrive at Norfolk Island, as pointed out above, but it is much too small and, of course, features a totally different colour scheme.

[4] In 1979 a sea serpent was sighted off Lower California by the crew of the *Granada*. What is relevant to our story, however, is that

[t]he ship's second officer recalled that he had seen a sea-serpent several yards long off Australia in 1871.[13]

That is not much to go on.

[5] However, in 1877 a very unusual creature was sighted in the Southern Ocean, for the chief officer of the *Maid of Judah* sent off the following memorandum, which was picked up by many Australian newspapers on Tuesday 4 December[14].

Tuesday, November 20, 1877 - Longitude 121 deg 26 min E., Latitude 40 deg 2 min S., at 11 a.m., while some of the hands were aloft they saw a very large serpent on the weather bow. The vessel passed close to it, about forty yards off, and it appeared to be about the length of the vessel. The head of this object appeared to be sunk down out of sight, while a good part of the body and tail was to be seen quite plainly. It was of a browny green colour, and did not appear to have any motion at the time of the vessel passing. There was a fresh gale blowing at the time, and a good deal of sea on, yet the thing was broadside on to the sea in curves, as if it was swimming, but the vessel was going faster, and so I could not see if it had any motion.

Some other papers[15] cited a length of 170 feet [52 metres], which was presumably the length of the ship. A long creature with no obvious head, fins, or paddles, moving sluggishly or not at all: when I read that I immediately recalled a chapter in Dr Roy

Mackal's book, *Searching for Hidden Animals*[16]. Firstly, you must understand that most of the large animals in the world, including us, are vertebrates ie they possess a backbone and internal skeleton. However, the vertebrates are only the major section of a larger group called the chordates, because there are smaller, rarer groups of animals with a more primitive body structure than the fishes, which possess a stiff rod called a notochord as a precursor to a backbone. One of these groups is the tunicates.

The tunicates are rather unusual. The larva are more like the ancestral chordate, tadpole-shaped with a notochord. But then they mature they change completely into filter feeders with hollow, barrel-shaped bodies featuring a mouth at one end and an anus at the other used to expel water. For this reason, many are known as "sea squirts". The important point is that many species are colonial and free-swimming. They are connected together, side by side, with their mouths all pointing outwards, and their anuses joining to form a common cavity or cloaca. Squirting water out of this common cavity allows the elongated colony to swim forward by jet propulsion. According to Dr Mackal, one species, *Pyrosoma spinosum* (now *Pyrostremma spinosusm*), the giant fire salp has been recorded as reaching a length of 10 metres, but it turns out this is a low measurement. According to Hamish Robertson[17], the open side of a 10.2 metre colony measured 1.2 metres across, but that colonies often possess a tail as long as the colony itself projecting from the rim. In other words, it would be 20 metres, or 66 feet long. It turns out, too, that these huge colonies are all from Australia and New Zealand, and he shows a photo of a diver riding one off Montague Island, near Newcastle.

But there's more. Another group of tunicates, the true salps reproduce in a rather unusual way. An asexual individual, called a stolon, buds off sexual individuals called gonozooids. However, these zooids remain attached to the stolon for a long time, as a chain. How long is, of course, impossible to gauge. The longest one would, by their nature, be the rarest, and the means of capturing them for study or measurement, such as trawling, would tend to break up the chain. Nevertheless, he claims that they may exceed 25 metres, or 82 feet.

In Dr Mackal's opinion, such gigantic chains might explain some rare sea serpent sightings, particularly one sighted by the crew of the *Nestor* off the coast of Malaya in 1892. In that case, it might be the best explanation for the *Maid of Judah* sighting, although 52 metres, assuming the estimate is correct, does sound excessive. Anyhow, it should serve to remind us that the world is a stranger place than most of us imagine.

[6] 1879 saw the appearance of two sea serpents on opposite sides of the continent. First of all, in early April, news of a sighting near Vasse, a small town close to Busselton, on Géographe Bay circulated through the Australian newspapers, of which this is typical:

WESTERN AUSTRALIA
Perth, April 5.
A report from Vasse states that a sea serpent about eighty feet [24 m] long has been seen there by a person of credibility. The head was about twenty feet [8 m] out of the water, and the body was two feet [60 cm] in diameter[18].

This is where brief reports such as this can be misleading. The overall impression here is that a long necked sea serpent stuck its head right up out of the water. However, the full story came out when a Colonial Surgeon, H. C. Barnett sent the witness's own statement to the scientific journal, *Nature*[19].

It turns out the "person of credibility" was the Rev. H. W. Brown, an educated chaplain of twenty-seven years in the colony, and "of whose accuracy there [could] be no question." The sighting was not at Vasse, but a short distance from Busselton, near Lockville, a place which no longer exists, but was then the site of a mill and wharf dealing with jarrah timber. Rev. Brown was riding home from Lockville along the beach when he met two friends, a Mr M'Guire and his wife walking in the opposite direction. The air was still, the sea as smooth as glass. Just a stone's throw from shore he saw a black log, almost end-on to him, when suddenly he noticed it was moving in the direction of Lockville, leaving a long, narrow wake behind it. Keeping abreast of it, he coo-eed to his friend M'Guire, only to notice that the sound had caused the animal to head seawards underwater. It then doubled back in-shore with the speed of a pike or swordfish, leaving the sudden change of direction plainly visible in the wake. Just as he caught up with M'Guire, the creature surfaced.

> ...when he was almost at rest, and all apparently was in view, I estimated the length to be 60 feet [18 m], straight and taper [*sic*], like a long spar, with the butt-end, his head and shoulders, showing well above the surface.
>
> I can only describe the head as like the end of a log, bluff, about two feet [60 cm] diameter; on the back we noticed, showing very distinctly above water, several square-topped fins.

The head, he claimed, bore little resemblance to a snake's, and he saw no lateral or tail fins.

The men and the monster parted company when it became to dark to observe. However, next day a fisherman called M'Mullan told him he had seen it 50 yards from the jetty, and considered it to be only 20 feet [6 m] long. Brown commented that it seemed the same length to him when it was in motion. Only when it came to rest did he realise its full size.

Rev. Brown was no artist, as can be seen from the sketch he left us (Fig 1).

Fig. 1. Rev. Brown's sketch of the Géographe Bay sea serpent.

[7] The next one was sighted on 27 July 1879 off Cape Howe, where the border between Victoria and New South Wales meets the sea. In fact, the short stretch of Victorian coastline before the border was to become the scene of quite a few sightings in later years.

You must remember that, in this period, communication between the states was mostly by sea rather than rail. So it was the the *Bosphorus* left Newcastle on 17July and arrived at Wallaroo Bay in South Australia on 10 August, upon which Captain Young announced what they had seen as they were rounding Cape Howe.

He says it had a head strongly resembling that of an ox, the likeness to which animal was somewhat increased by its having two protuberances resembling horns on its forehead; its length was about thirty feet [9 m], and its diameter about 3 feet, the body being brown, and apparently without scales. It remained near the vessel for a considerable time, and was the object of much interest and speculation to the crew of the '*Bosphorus*'[20].

Nobody seems to have asked the captain for any additional details. I would like to have known whether it stuck its head out of the water like a periscope, because a pair of protuberances is a feature of many long necked sea serpent reports.

After that, we had a rest for another decade. When the gay nineties arrived, however, they came in with a roar.

3. The Fabulous, Fantastic Moha-Moha

[8] Miss Selina Lovell (1827-1905) was born in London and came to Australia at the age of 36, along with her brother[21]. She soon took up school teaching in southeast Queensland, and in 1880 she was posted to the school serving the small white community around the Sandy Cape Lighthouse at the northern tip of Fraser Island. Amicable, timid, and a little eccentric, she was also known as a keen amateur botanist, who discovered three previously undescribed plants, two of which now bear her name. Then, in June 1890 she allegedly saw something extraordinary which also ended up being named after her.

The story was originally published in the British journal, *Land and Water* on 3 January 1891, when a letter and sketch by Miss Lovell was submitted by a "constant reader" who self-identified by the Latin phrase, TEMPUS OMNIA MONSTRAT, or "Time reveals everything". According to Miss Lovell's undated missive[22]:

We have had a visit from a monster turtle fish. I send a sketch of it. It let me stand for half an hour within five feet [1½ m] of it. When tired of my looking at it, it put its large neck and head into the water and swept around seaward, raising its huge dome-shaped body about five feet out of water, and put its twelve feet [3.6 m] of fish-like tail over the dry shore, elevating it at an angle. Then, giving its tail a half twist, it shot off like a flash of lightning, and I saw its tail in the air about a quarter of a mile [0.4 km] off, where the steamers anchor.

It has either teeth or serrated jaw-bones. Native blacks call it "Moka Moka," and say they like to eat it, and that it has legs and fingers. I did not see its legs, as they were in the water. What I saw of it was about 27 ft. or 28ft. [3.2 - 3.5 m], but I think it must be 30 ft. in all. Whilst it head was out of water it kept its mouth open, and, as I could not see any nostrils, I fancy it breathes through its mouth. The jaws are about 18 in. [46 cm] in length; the head and neck greenish white, with large white spots on the neck, and a band of white round a very black eye and round upper and lower jaws.

The body was dome-shaped, about 8 ft. [2.4 m] across and 5ft. [1½ m] high, smooth, and slate-grey in colour. Tail about 12 ft. [3.6 m], the fish part wedge-shaped, and fin of chocolate brown. Then beautiful silver shading to white scales size of thumb nail.

Also in the letter, but not normally reported, Miss Lovell described a creature called a "womang", which can be identified as a manta ray, thus confirming her powers of observation and description[23].

A comment by the editor of *Land and Water* expressing doubts about the story provoked a letter from Miss Lovell dated 4 March 1891, and published in the issue of 25 April.

I received from my sister your account and drawing of the *Moha Moha*, which is not correctly drawn. I send a rough sketch. . . .

This is what makes me believe that TEMPUS OMNIA MONSTRAT was her sister. You will note that the name of the animal has been changed from "moka moka". As will be shown later, an independent letter in February also used that term, which is almost certainly the correct form. Aboriginal languages lack the sound of "h", so "moha moha" is impossible for them to pronounce. Equally, it is difficult to pronounce in English if stressed on the first syllable, so it is unlikely that an English speaking hoaxer would invent it. I presume that the new term resulted from a printer's error, or a misreading of the author's handwriting. In any case, it stuck, and "moha moha" is how it is known in all subsequent discussions. But to continue, Miss Lovell explained that:

The tail was over the dry shore for half an hour, so close to me, that five footsteps would have enabled me to put my hand upon it.

Also -

The blacks, who had not seen it on the day I did, named it once from my sketch, which must, therefore, be pretty accurate, and called it "Moha, Moha," and laughed and said "Saucy fellow, Meebee," in English, "dangerous turtle."

"It is eight years since it attacked the blacks' camp. It can stand upright, and it put its legs on the shoulders of a powerful black, 6 ft. [1.8 m] high, and knocked him down. That year it

invaded their camp, and nearly caught one man by the leg. For
months after the blacks camped inland. . . .   It is not a turtle, but a
monster, half fish, half tortoise, with the carapace perfectly round
in front.

The story must have come to the attention of Dr William
Saville-Kent, a British marine biologist who was, at the time,
Commissioner of Fisheries for Queensland, and later Western
Australia, for he wrote to Miss Lovell and incorporated her reply
into his tome, *The Great Barrier Reef of Australia*[24]. Although the
subject was introduced in a light-hearted, even facetious manner,
he did attempt to immortalise her by naming the beast,
Chelosauria Lovelli, which means "*Mr*. Lovell's turtle lizard". Yes,
this learned man of science had been so used to seeing Latinised
men's names included in zoological nomenclature that he forget
that his correspondent was female. The specific name should have
been *lovellae*. Also, the use of a capital letter was incorrect. The
specific name is never capitalised, even when based on a proper
name. Such an error in common among journalists, but one is
surprised to find it in a scientific publication. In any case, the name
is not valid, because there was no physical specimen lodged for it
to refer to[25]. However, let us record Miss Lovell's exact words.

I was (while walking on the Sandy Island beach) admiring the
stillness of the sea, it being a dead calm, when my eye caught sight
of the head and neck of a creature I had never seen before. I went
to the edge of the water and saw a huge animal, lying at full length,
which was not at all disturbed by my close proximity to it,
enabling me to observe the glossy skin of the head and neck,
smooth and shiny as satin. Its great mouth was wide open all the
time it was out of the water. In about a quarter of an hour or so it
put its head and neck slowly into the sea, closing its jaws as it did
so. I then saw what a long neck it had, as it moved round in a half
circle, and also perceived that the head and neck were moving
under a carapace. When the head was pointing out to sea it rose up,
putting a long wedge-shaped tail out of the water over the dry
shore, parallel to myself, and not more than five feet from me, not
touching the sand, but elevated. I could have stood under the
'flukes of its tail'.

The only part of the body that had marks like joints (like in size and shape to a common brick) was also on the dry shore, but *resting* on the sand; the great dome-shaped carapace, dull slate-grey, was standing quite five feet high, and so hid its long neck and head from my view, which before it rose I could see as a long shadow in the water. The carapace was smooth and without marks of any sort. The fish-like part of the tail was as glossy and shiny as the head and neck, but of a beautiful silver-grey, shading to white, with either markings or large scales, each bordered with a ridge of white, but if scales, not like those of a fish in position, as the fishes' lie horizontally, whilst the Moha's, if scales, lie perpendicularly, each the size of a man's thumb-nail. It had a thick fleshy fin near the end, about three feet [90 cm] from the flukes, and, like them, chocolate-brown. The flukes were semi-transparent; I could see the sun shining through them, showing all the bones very forked. One of the girls asked me if a shark had bitten a piece out of its tail, and the other one wanted to know if I thought it was an alligator! The fish-like part was quite twelve feet long.

All the time the animal was on shore it was perfectly motionless; at least it gave a curious half-twist to the fluke part of its tail, the movement only reaching just beyond the fleshy fin, and, without disturbing the water in the slightest degree, vanished. I seemed only to have taken one breath when I saw its tail out of the water abut the same place where the steamer anchors, sending a quantity of fish into the air. I then saw it give a twist of its tail and it disappeared altogether. The black boy saw it on shore the previous Monday, the 9th inst. As I was so close to it for at least half an hour, I was able to study its shape and colouring. In moving about, head and tail were seen alternately above water, but not even the shadow of the great body, and, from the length of that a spectator could not guess that the head and tail belonged to the same creature, particularly as the colouring is so different. The parts I did not see were the legs. I stooped down and tried, but in vain, to see them, though the Moha was only standing in a foot of water, but the Black described them as being like an alligator. I wrote to Dr. Ramsay (Sydney) to ask if the Moha was the same creature as the great turtle of New Guinea, of which the Sydney Museum possesses a skeleton, but he said in reply that it was quite unlike, and calls the Moha a tortoise, which I think is correct.

Dr. Günther (of the British, Natural History, Museum) would give £100 for the entire animal, £50 for part, and a fair price for the head and neck sun-dried.

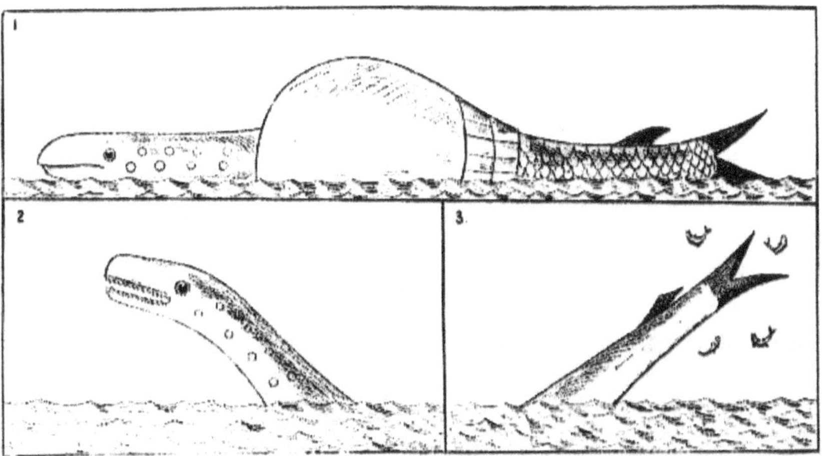

Fig. 2. Miss Lovell's three sketches of the Moha-Moha, as published by Saville-Kent.
1. The animal lying prone in shallow water.
2. The animal with head reared above the water, the body and tail being submerged.
3. The tail raised above water, and by its actions scattering a shoal of fishes.

In response to Saville-Kent's request for corroborative testimony, the following certificate was included:

> We, the undersigned, saw the Moha-Moha (as described by Miss Lovell) making for the shore of Sandy Cape on June 8th, 1890:
>> James Alsbury, 1st assistant, Sandy Cape Lighthouse.
>> William H. Lees, 3rd assistant, Sandy Cape Lighthouse.
>> Mrs. Lees.
>> Donald Henderson.
>> Jemima Alsbury
>> Jessie Alsbury

The last two were listed as daughters of James Alsbury.

The black boy, Robert added his mark, for he had seen the animal the previous Monday, and he and the Alsbury girls had been with Miss Lovell when she saw the moha moha.

Some confusion exists as to the date. Miss Lovell claimed that Robert had seen it "the previous Monday, the 9th inst." but failed to state the month. However, Gould[26] correctly pointed out that the 9th did not fall on a Monday in 1890 in any month but June. The 8th June, of course, was a Sunday, an ideal day to walk along the beach, for there would have been no school. Magin[27] suggested that the word "previous" referred to the date of writing the report. However, the report was written ten months after the event. It is hard to avoid the conclusion that someone has mixed up the dates.

As a youngster, when I first heard about the moha moha, I was very excited. I would like to believe it. Nevertheless, one must accept that the fact that nothing like this has ever been reported before or since is a strong argument against its authenticity.

Just the same, one must also admit that the lady had been very detailed and consistent in her description of the animal, and its movements, but what sort of animal does the description imply? The tail clearly is that of a fish - and not just any fish, but the teleosts, or modern ray-finned fish, which encompass most of the fish of the world outside of sharks and rays. The "flukes" at the end, and the rayed fin on top give it away. And the fact that the "flukes" were vertical means that it must swim by horizontal undulations of the tail. However, Heuvelmans has made the obvious point[28] that vertical scales make no sense on a body part that must flex horizontally. In order for them not to impede motion, they must be in transverse rows which slip easily each another. He also pointed out that she would have to have been very short-sighted if, at a distance of a meter and a half, she could not tell whether they were scales or markings.

Although the tail belonged to a fish, no fish has a true neck or feet like an alligator's. The front part was very obviously that of a tortoise. Miss Lovell was right; it was a combination of fish and tortoise. This is impossible.

There are a number of other things which don't ring true. For a start, although it was usual at this period to refer to crocodiles as alligators - hence the Alligator Rivers in the Northern Territory - their southern distribution is normally reckoned as Gladstone. Only the occasional stray turns up at Fraser Island. So would the black boy even be familiar with the English term? Would he not have compared its feet to (say) that of a fresh water tortoise?

Secondly, I am familiar with Fraser Island although I will admit I haven't been as far north as Sandy Cape. My experience has been that the eastern beaches are under constant assault from endless rows of breakers which roll in without ceasing from the vast Pacific. I won't say that completely calm days never occur, only that they would be extremely rare. To be fair, it probably would be on such a day that a marine monster would come inshore. More to the point, the slope of the beach is very slight, for the island is essentially one huge sandbar. You would have to wade out a long way to get into deep water.

Miss Lovell's account is confusing. She obviously should not have been teaching English composition. (What, for example, is meant by saying the tail was "parallel to myself"?) However, she claimed that, after it "moved around in a half circle", its head was facing out to sea. Therefore, when she first saw it with its head and neck out of the water and its great body just a shadow in the water, the head and neck must have been parallel to the shore. Also, it couldn't have been more than three or four metres from the shore, since, when it turned, its tail was over the dry land. It was now in only a foot (30 cm) of water, but previously, the carapace was hidden under water. The bottom must have dropped abruptly very close to the shore. Based on the topography of the island, I do not believe there is any place where this can occur.

Next, she said she could have stood under the flukes, so we must assume that the tail must have been elevated at an angle to a level of at least a metre and a half, and held it there for a long time, estimated at a quarter of an hour (originally she said half an hour).

With all due respect, this is a very peculiar thing for a marine animal to do. I also have difficult in imaging why, in swimming, it would would erect its tail and head alternately above water.

Then there is the fact that, although it has never been seen again, it was an occasional visitor to the island (but nowhere else), because, in her first article, she claimed the Aborigines liked to eat it. Yet in the second article she said the blacks camped inland for several months because it had attacked their camp. The statement that it put its forefeet on the shoulders of one of the men is the last straw which breaks the back of credibility. All this shouts: "Hoax!"

It is easy to see how it developed. Probably, she wrote the original letter for *Land and Water* as a joke, but when Saville-Kent approached her, she felt she had to keep it up. She then asked the staff at the lighthouse to join her in the joke, for who doesn't like the idea of putting a bit over one of the eggheads? At least she should be complimented on the way she maintained the consistency of her story and description, albeit not always coherently.

At least, that's what I *would* have said. However, recently new information has been uncovered by Ulrich Magin[29]. Although Saville-Kent had stated that "full publicity was given to Miss Lovell's narrative in the contemporary newspapers", neither Magin nor I have been able to locate any using the search engine on Trove. However, he did establish that Miss Lovell did write to the Government Commissioner at Thursday Island on 10 February 1891 i.e. shortly after her first article in *Land and Water*, and the letter was published in the *Torres Straits Gazette*. I have been unable to access this newspaper, but Magin did discover an article in the *Auckland Star* (New Zealand) of 18 April 1891.

> About the best great sea-serpent yarn we have heard for a long time is narrated by Captain Charles Nightingall, of the steamer Norkoowa, of Melbourne, now in port here. Captain Nightingall's veracity, etc. etc., in unquestioned, so that our readers may accept the tale without any "doots" whatever - if they choose. This gentleman obtained his information from the most reliable sources while on a trip some three weeks ago from

Newcastle up to Thursday Island, in Torres Strait. The story has as yet only been published in one newspaper, the "Torres Straits Gazette," of Thursday Island, so that it has the merit of being new as well as "strictly truthfl." When the Norkoowa was at Thursday Island, Capt. Nightingall was given by Sir John Douglas, the local Queensland Government Commissioner, the following copy of a letter received from a locality down the coast.

"Sandy Cape, February 10th, 1891. Sir Douglas Sir, - Will you kindly get some one or other of your subordinates to inquire among the captains of coasting and pearling vessels, if the very large turtle, a new kind found North, at all resembles the animal of which a rude sketch is inclosed. This creature was on shore on two days in June at Sandy Cape. The colouring and shape were sufficiently accurate for the animal to be recognised and named by some of the blacks, who did not see it either day. They called it the moka moka [*sic*] - I am, etc., S. Lovell, Provisional School." W.T. Sandy Cape.

Miss Lovell is the schoolmistress, and also postmistress, and several other "officials" at Sandy Cape (Queensland). She enclosed with her letter elaborate sketches of the animal referred to, which Captain Nightingall evidently devoted several days of his time to copying and touching up for he has drafted some excellent sketches of the great sea-serpent in question. The sketches are in three sections. The first represents a crocodile-like reptile with a square-cut wall-sided face somewhat like that of the sperm-whale, of a dirty yellow colour; two large eyes; and a mouth, armed with a terrific-looking set of teeth, always open when out of the water. The last or tail end of the creature is about the same length as the other end, with a wedge-shaped tail like a dugong and evidently coloured with very fishy-looking scales, colour light blue, but with tail dirty red. The middle or back of the creature is, however, a mystery. The two sections described one could almost understand as those of a monster sea snake of variegated colours, but the connecting section is what bothered the enterprising "schoolmarm," Sir Douglas, Capt. Nightingall, and also ourselves. The two ends are connected by a "great domed scarapace [sic]," to use the words accompanying the sketch, being in the form of a turtle with a back about six feet high. This domed back is of a dull slate grey, without marks until near the junction with the tail section. When the creature stood up it was five or six feet high; when lying full length the feet - for it had feet also - were not seen. The Queensland blacks state that it was rather over 36 feet long, and blacks are not given to romancing, owing to want of civilisation presumably. Its feet are those of a crocodile. In moving through the water the animal's head first goes down and the tail raises, and *vice versa*. . . .

You will notice some differences in the colour scheme from that provided to Dr. Saville-Kent. It would have been useful to read the original *Torres Straits Gazette* article, to see the drawings, and determined whether the colours were described in words, or whether the letter to Sir Douglas contained coloured drawings.

But the important thing is the act of writing for information to the Government representative in Thursday Island just after the publication of the *Land and Water* article is not what would be expected of a hoaxer. It is more consistent with a person who honestly believes her own story, and hopes to solve the mystery. Ditto her writing to the Sydney Museum and the British Natural History Museum. Also, it appears the original publication was based on a letter to her sister. And, of course, there are the alleged witnesses among the Fraser Island community.

But the story cannot be true.

4. Sea Serpents in the Nineties

[9] If the moha-moha had really appeared on Sunday 8 June 1890, then it was beaten by a sea serpent which appeared off the east coast of Victoria the previous Sunday afternoon. The steamer *Victorian*, sailing from Sydney, arrived in Melbourne the following morning, and Captain Lockyer told his story[30]. The sea had been as smooth as glass when they saw it a short distance from the ship: jet black from head to tail, an estimated 80 feet [26 m] long and 6 feet [1.8 m] in circumference (he probably meant diameter). All of the passengers watched its gambols as it "sported itself high above the steamer" - which suggests it was one of the "long necked" variety - and they demanded he give it a wide berth.

Interestingly, the captain said it resembled one which had passed him two years before but 80 miles, or approximately 130 km to the south, ie somewhere near the entrance to Bass Strait.

[10] November 1891 brought in two dramas. The first was a farce involving a supposedly dead bishop, a supposedly dead sea serpent, and the most prestigious newspaper in England[31]. On the 6th of the month *The Times* announced the death of the Bishop of Adelaide, the Rt. Rev. Dr. G. W. Kennion. Three days later, however, it was forced to print a retraction, because His Grace had informed them that his obituary had been somewhat premature. I doubt if he had even been sick. Another two days elapsed before they explained the cause of their mistake. It turned out that Dalziel's News Agency had received a cablegram from an Australian agent:

> 'INFLUENZA EXTENSIVELY PREVALENT WALES VICTORIA NUMEROUS DEATHS BISHOP ADELAIDE FOUND DEAD SEA SERPENT SIXTY FEET COFFIN BAY'

You will notice that the absence of punctuation, as well as the obtuseness of the subject, rendered the passage somewhat ambiguous. *The Times* decided that last six words made no obvious sense but, in any case, they did not belong to the previous four words. Now they understood that they must have been connected, and that the Bishop of Adelaide, or possible someone called *Mr. Bishop*, must have found what he believed was a dead sea serpent.

Finally, some Australian newspapers arrived, and they reported that the Bishop of Adelaide had written to a friend describing how, at Avoid Point, near Coffin Bay, South Australia, he had come across a dead sea serpent 60 feet [18 m] long, with a snakelike head 5 feet [1½ m] long, with two blowholes in the top but no teeth in the jaws. It had a tail like a whale. It was the most peculiar animal he had ever seen.

Or had he? The following year brought the publication of, Oudemans' book, *The Great Sea-Serpent*[32], which recorded it as a hoax on page 574 because a Mr. Gilbert Bogle of Newcastle-on-Tyne had written to the bishop, who replied that the story was false.

It is interesting that everybody seems to have assumed that the bishop must have belonged to the Church of England, forgetting that Adelaide had enough Roman Catholics to justify a bishop of their own. If so, however, he failed to come forward and take credit for the discovery.

So what did the Australian press actually say? Let me be the first to reproduce a typical article, in particular, that of the *Evening News* (Sydney), Friday 6 November 1891 (the same date as *The Times'* article) on page 5.

The Sea Serpent Found at Last

A BISHOP THE DISCOVER

Adelaide, Friday.- A remarkable discovery of a sea serpent is reported. The Bishop of Adelaide, writing from Avoid Point, near Coffin Bay, to a friend here, says that while riding along the sea beach he came across a dead sea serpent. The animal was about 60 feet long, and had a head 5 feet long, like that of an enormous snake, with two blowholes on the top. There were no teeth in the jaws. The body was round, and the tail resembled that of a whale. The bishop says it was the most extraordinary animal he ever beheld. As this discovery is vouched for by a bishop, there will be some inclination to believe that the sea serpent has been found at last.

At once, you might notice a few things missing from the story:

- the name of the bishop;
- his denomination;
- when this was supposed to have happened. Coffin Bay is a long way from Adelaide, near the southwest tip of the Eyre Peninsula, but not too far from the larger town of Port Lincoln. Still, a bishop might visit there as part of his circuit. I don't know what the mail system was like at the time, but it is possible a ship regularly plied between Port Lincoln and Adelaide, carrying the mail. However, the fact that the bishop allegedly wrote to his friend suggests he intended to stay on the peninsula for some time, yet he was easily contacted from England when the story broke.
- Finally, the name of the friend who broke the story to the anonymous journalist. Did he show him the letter?

Personally, I cannot see that there is any value in this story. It is known that the decaying carcass of a basking shark can look like a plesiosaur, but the fact that the bishop denied the story to Mr. Bogle suggests it was completely bogus - assuming he got the right bishop.

[11] What happened on 17 November that year in Newcastle harbour was not a farce but high drama. Around about noon, a diver belonging to the Harbours and Rivers Department was working at the mooring of No.1 buoy in about 30 feet [9 metres] of water, when he suddenly signaled to be brought up. Once back on the pontoon, as his companions removed his helmet, he appeared faint. As he explained, while he was working at the stated depth,

he observed an enormous object approaching him which at first seemed like a dark cloud. As it came closer he perceived a huge sea monster fully 30ft long, with a bulldog-shaped head, sharp piercing eyes, and a savage mouth. It seemed to be extremely flat, with two large fins flapping, and swam along quietly, but determinedly[33].

Now, it is not stated what was the clarity of the water at that depth, but it occurs to me that unless visibility was greater than 30 feet, or 9 metres, it would have been difficult to have seen the whole of the monster all at once. First the head would have come into view, and have vanished by the time the tail appeared, and it must have been very close indeed. This would have made it all the more terrifying. (Of course, if it were clear enough to be seen all at once, then one might suspect that his team members on the pontoon would have been able to see both him and the animal.) Water tends to act as a magnifying glass, as does fear, but even taking that into consideration, the size was huge. Normally only sharks come anywhere near half that size, and the diver claimed to be fully familiar with sharks and whales, as well he might. As far as bony fish go, an oarfish might fit the size limit, and a marlin can reach five metres, but the front end of both are quite distinct, and different from that described. It sounds like nothing more than a gigantic eel.

There is more. While he was relating his adventure, the monster rose to the surface close to the pontoon. The group set off in pursuit in two boats, but although they stabbed it several times with boathooks, it made no difference. Eventually, when the creature was off the lifeboat shed, "it leisurely turned its head, and after surveying its pursuers dived down and was seen no more." Their description matched that of the diver who, for some reason, refused to return to the water that day.

There's more. On Saturday 5 December another monster appeared in Newcastle harbour[34]. The tugboat, *Gamocock* was being hoisted onto a slip when two men called Brinkworth and Emslie saw a huge fish floundering in shallow water, and immediately set out after it armed with a joiner's adze. (They must have been really hard up for weapons.) Brinkworth stabbed it in the fin, upon which the implement held fast, and a flip of the fin by the fish hurled him into the water. However, with Emslie holding on to Brinkworth, and Brinkworth onto the adze, and with the tide going out, the fish was caught on the sand. After assistance arrived, the fish was towed round to Stockton wharf and hoisted onto a large pontoon. For the next two days it was put on display at the Market wharf, and was said to have gained the owners "a small fortune" in admission fees.

Its measurements were determined to be: diameter 12 feet [3.6 m], length 9 feet [2.7 m], thickness 3 feet [90 cm], and weight approximately 1½ tonnes. You might be surprised to read that the diameter was greater than the length, but this was a species of sunfish, must likely the ocean sunfish, *Mola mola*. The heaviest of all the bony fish, it is nevertheless one of the weirdest in shape. It looks like a swimming head detached from the body of a much larger fish, and much more at home in the open ocean than inshore.

That story reached the news stand on the Monday. The very next day brought the headline: 'The sea monster's mate captured[35]'. What made them think sunfish have mates? Well, apparently it was "known by nautical men" that they tended to travel in pairs, so many of them set out to look for the second one on Monday. About dinner time one of them was discovered near the entrance to the Hunter River, where it was chased by a crew of pilot boatmen, who managed to capture it with a boathook and, after a fierce struggle, tow it to shore. Once there, it was haggled over by a team of speculative watermen, who purchased it, erected a tent at Market wharf, and charged the public for the privilege of viewing it. Now, apart from the fact that the females are larger than the males, I have no idea how to distinguish the sexes of ocean sunfish, because I am not an ichthyologist. On the other hand, neither was anybody else in the picture at the time, but despite the absence of such expert advice, the newspaper assured us that the first specimen captured was a male, and the second a female - its mate, of course. The last word was that the owners of both specimens planned to have them stuffed and mounted somewhere. I wonder whether that ever happened.

[12] Montague Island lies off the southeast coast of New South Wales, at 36° 15'S, 150° 13'E, and thus ideally placed to intercept any ship travelling between Newcastle and Melbourne. Thus it was that, when the steamer *Industry* arrived at the latter city in April 1893, they told the following story[36]:

"At 2.30 p.m. on the 25th ult., [ie March]" runs the narrative, "when the ship was about 10 miles [16 km] north of Montague Island, and about 6 miles from the land, a sea serpent rose out of the water about 200 yards from the vessel, which was going at about 10 miles an hour. As it rose it caused a great commotion, and when about 15 feet [4½ m] above the surface it commenced swinging its head about after the manner of the giants in a pantomime. The eyes and ears were very large, and the portion of the body out of the water was covered by large scales of a dirty brown and white color. Three times it rose in 10 minutes, and then swam away towards the shore, leaving a ripple behind it."

When an animal's head and neck towers out of the water and swings around, it is hard to identify it with any fish or whale. This is another example of a long-necked sea serpent, although normally the creature is not described as possessing scales.

[13] Getting back to Newcastle, we discover that something very strange was happening in the adjacent waters on Saturday 25 August 1894. Several residents believed they had watched a sea serpent chase a whale. Initially, when an object was seen repeatedly rising and coming down with great force and lots of splashing, the observers, who were positioned on the old Gaol Hill, thought they were observing a battle between a whale and a thrasher shark. However, about 4 p.m., they saw a large black object heading swiftly in the direction of Nobby's (a short peninsula), followed furiously by another, which was repeatedly raising its head 6 or 7 feet [1.8 - 2.1 m] out of the water and attacking the other. When they came abreast of the old Gaol Hill, they passed within half a mile [800 metres] of the beach.

It was then seen that the second monster was not a thrasher shark. The first was a whale, there could be little doubt, as it was large and bulky, and almost black in color. The second had a serpentine head with a brownish-colored back and silvery belly. This was distinctly seen when it raised part of its body out of the water[37].

I don't know what to make of this. Multiple witnesses are unlikely to be making it all up. However, the distance was very great, even granted that estimates of distances and size are highly unreliable at sea. At the same time, it is hard to see how they would have been mistaken about a serpentine neck raised out of the water and striking another animal, and that does not sound like any sea creature known to science. As we shall see, a few years later an encounter between a sea serpent and a whale was reported from the opposite side of the continent.

[14] Two years later another sea serpent turned up on the opposite side of the continent. On 3 October the steamer, *Echuca* was returning from India with a cargo of 540 camels, of which all but two survived, and was about 50 miles, or 80 km, off Fremantle when several crew members saw something nearly 100 feet [30 metres] long and of great girth. At first they thought it was a whale, but changed their minds when it raised above the water a head "almost a facsimile of an abnormal cobra.[38]" Again, we have a long-necked sea serpent, but how we wish the journalist had asked a few questions, such as the distance, length of observation, colour, presence or absence of humps, etc., etc.

As an example of the popular state of mind at the time, we might jump forward to an amusing incident on New Year's Day, 1910. An unnamed person found a bottle on the beach at Beachport in southeast South Australia. It was much discoloured, and may well have been fourteen years old, and when it was broken, lo and behold! There was a message dated November 16, 1896.

"We have seen this day and enormous sea-serpent, and lost two of our mess. The serpent measured from nose to tail 50 ft. 6 in."
Signed F. R.McPhie, A. H. Jennings, A. Lucas, 'H.M.S.
Protector'"[39]

Of course, the press did not take the message seriously, although they agreed that the date might have been genuine. I might add that although the Royal Navy has possessed, at one time or another, seven ships named H.M.S. *Protector*, none existed in the period 1864 to 1945[40].

[15] The following year the scene switched back to the east coast again. This time, in the morning of 29 June 1897, the steam tug, *Hero* was operating about 25 miles [40 km] east of Botany Heads, when Captain H. Penner happened to see something like a huge snake coiled in a figure 8 shape close to the boat, apparently asleep. It was multicoloured and seemed to be covered with scales. When they approached closer, it uncoiled itself and moved away until, about half a mile [800 metres] away, it suddenly disappeared. It was estimated to be 30 or 40 feet [9 to 12 metres] long, as thick as a man's thigh in the middle, tapering to the tail, with a head twice the width of a large human hand[41].

This is puzzling, for it was obviously some sort of snake, but much bigger than any sea snake. And, in case anyone asks, we do not have any land pythons of that size, nor as they prone to sleeping at sea.

[16] The next encounter is really interesting and dramatic, and took place at the mouth of the Huon River in Tasmania, slightly north of tiny Huon Island. For your reference, this island is situated at 43° 17½' S, 147° 09' E. As an example of the how the press worked in those days, the story was first published[42] on 3 August 1899, and was picked up verbatim by other newspapers on 4, 14, and 24 August, and on 1st September. It is best to quote the entire article.

A curious experience is related by Mr Robert Bowman, a fisherman, residing at Garden Island Creek (Tas.) He states that about 4 p.m. on Tuesday, July 25, he was returning to Garden Island Creek from Huon Island in a small punt, and when off the north point of Charlotte Cove, about a mile [1.6 km] below the Garden Island Creek jetty, he heard a splashing noise in the water ahead of him. Upon looking round, he saw some creature in the water which was quite unknown to him. It had, when first seen, elevated a long neck about 20ft [6 m] out of the water, with a triangular-shaped flat head bent at right angles to the neck, and seemed, from its actions, to have been feeding on something. The long neck was very black, and rather shiny on the back part, but lighter underneath, and appeared to swell out rather suddenly where it reached the water. Mr Bowman says that he did not notice how long the head was, as his whole attention was concentrated upon getting away as fast as he could, but he thought it was about 3 ft [90 cm] broad. Watching the creature whilst rowing away from it, he noticed it bend down its neck, and protrude a small portion of its tail from the water, and then 'bend its body into a bow', as he describes. From the head to the end of the tail he estimates the creature as about 30ft [9 m] long as a rough guess, but thinks it might have been more. As soon as the creature caught sight of the punt it started to follow it, but Mr Bowman states that at the time he was close to land, and immediately pulled inside the heavy fringe of kelp that extends along the rocky shore, with a view to landing. He found, however, that the 'beast', as he calls it, would not venture the kelp. It tried several times and dived but always returned to the outside of the belt. It followed him for a quarter of a mile [400 metres] before giving up the chase. Mr. Bowman states that when swimming after him it carried its head 4ft or 5ft [1.2 to 1.5 metres] above the water, and made at times bursts of speed that sent the water flying from its neck like that from the bows of a fast steamer. He does not think it was capable of keeping up a high speed for any length of time. Mr Bowman was shown the pictures of some ancient saurians in the 'Century Magazine' of November, 1897, which a resident happened to possess, and immediately lighted on the representation of a 'plesiosaurus,' with the remark, 'That's the beast all right.' He stated, however, that he did not notice any paddles or fins, as the body was under water, but thinks that the neck and head, as shown in the picture, almost exactly represent the neck and head of the creature he saw. Having been a fisherman for many years, Mr Bowman says that he is familiar with all the whales, sharks, and seals found in these waters, and could not have mistaken one of them for a sea serpent. While swimming after him, it moved its head from side to side with a serpentine motion. With a companion he went on the following day to try if he could see it again, but failed to do so.

On has to admire his courage in venturing out the following day to look for it. The description fits the "long necked" sea serpent very well. However, if the neck were really 20 feet long, with a swelling at the base where it joined the body, it is likely it was a lot longer than 30 feet. On the other hand, the fact that it was held only 4 to 5 feet out of the water when chasing him suggests that the original estimate was an exaggeration.

[17] It is likely that, were it not for the publicity afforded the previous sighting, the following one wouldn't have been reported. It took place in Bass Strait, but when the *Hampton* arrived in port on 9 August, Captain M'Donald gave the following account.

"On August 1st, in latitude 30.50 degrees south, and longitude 148.23 degrees east, at 9.40 a.m., the ship, while close hauled on the starboard tack, with a moderate breeze, clear weather, and smooth sea, my attention was drawn by the chief officer and helmsman to a strange-looking creature in the water about 10 yards from the ship. It was 20 feet [6 metres] or, perhaps, more in length, and from four to five feet [1.2 to 1.5 metres] in girth. It was a reddish brown color, with a head and body resembling a snake. No fins were visible. The monster was stationary at the time on the weather quarter, and did not attempt to move as the ship passed."[43]

The chief officer corroborated his captain's story, and added that the head resembled the fluke of a ship's anchor, and that the tail tapered to a point. However, he claimed that the width of the animal was between two and three feet [60 and 90 cm]. It's a point in favour of authenticity that the two witnesses provided slightly different descriptions. It certainly sounds like some large snake, but it might have been a huge eel.

That was the end of sightings for the 1890s. The following year was to provide something even more spectacular.

5. The Early Twentieth Century

All right, strictly speaking, the twentieth century did not commence until 1901, but let us not be too pedantic. The important thing is that in the second half of 1900 newspapers all over the continent - big dailies and little regional rags - were agog with the tale of two incidents which took place close together near the southwest tip of Western Australia.

[18] On Wednesday 15 August the S.S. *Perth* docked at Fremantle, where Captain Campbell reported what they had seen at 8 o'clock that morning, just outside Fremantle[44]: a serpentine animal with a white body and a black head, the latter of of which was raised 20 feet [6 metres] out of the water, but its total length could not be ascertained. It appeared to be attacking a whale, and both were in sight for about an hour.

A fortnight later, the ship was docked in Melbourne, and since interest was still running high, a reporter interviewed the captain and obtained full details.

You must understand that I wasn't the first man aboard to observe the 'serpent.' The steamer was returning from Geraldton to Fremantle on the 15th inst., and we were having a nice fair-weather run. At about 8 a.m., when we were between Cape Leschenault and Wreck Island, about 12 miles [19 km] off land and 35 miles [56 km] north of Rottnest Island, the chief officer, Mr. Neale, who was on the bridge, saw the giraffe-like object upreared vertically from the surface of the ocean, and immediately he rushed to me and reported that there was some unseemly monster disporting itself about 100 yards away from the vessel. Eager to see what the creature was, I at once ran up to the bridge, and, after waiting a couple of minutes, saw the uncanny creature raise its head and body 20 ft. out of the water. It would remain in that position for about a minute, and then disappear. This pastime it indulged in most regularly for a long time. A small whale, too, occasionally made its appearance, and appeared to be at war with the other monster. I noticed that the whale never appeared above water during the time the sea serpent was visible. They seemed to take turn about in coming above and going under the water. I watched their manoeuvres for fully a quarter of an hour, and then went down to breakfast, but several of my crew and some of the passengers who were on deck watched the serpent and the whale for a full hour. A good view of them was to be obtained from the boatskids. As far as I could judge with the aid of my binocular, the monster appeared to be 6 ft. [1.8 m] in breadth, with a flattish body, and the head and scales seemed to be similar to those of a snake. The head was black and small, and, like that of the ordinary reptile, falling away at the neck and widening at the body, which was white. During the time the monster's head and body were visible it lashed the water into foam. Both of them were travelling in a southerly direction …[45]

Again, we have a long-necked sea serpent, and a fairly large one at that, if its head could be raised 6 metres above the water. However, a white body with a black head is something unusual, and most such sea serpents are not described as possessing scales.

[19] The S.S. *Nemesis* was a steamer which used to trade between Sydney and Perth. On 11 October 1900, just as she was about to commence its eastward journey, her Captain Laurence Thomson told Captain Abrahams, the Harbour Master at Bunbury, that the ship had encountered a sea serpent between Vasse and Cape Naturaliste[46]. Resembling a serpent 200 feet [60 m] long, it moved rapidly over the sea the way a snake progresses on land, at the same time continually lashing the water with a very flexible fin 30 feet [9 m] long. Since he claimed to have discussed the matter with Captain Campbell of the *Perth*, the reporter interviewed Captain Campbell, who said he believed that the two of them has seen the same creature.

Such was the rather brief record provided by the press. No questions were asked about any extra details of its anatomy, the names of any other witnesses, or even when it all took place. Not to worry, for the previous two years a monthly journal had existed which encouraged members of the public to relate their own adventures: *The Wide World Magazine*, which continued until 1965, long enough for yours truly to become enamoured of it. (I still collect any edition I can lay my hands of.) Featuring authors as famous as Arthur Conan Doyle, Ion Idriess, Henry Morton Stanley, and Albert Schweitzer, it even provided the "scoop" of Butch Cassidy's death in Bolivia. Authors were required to affirm that their stories were true in every detail, and most of them, I suspect, were. Nevertheless, no method existed of confirming their accuracy, and hoaxes were known to have crept in.

Captain Thomson appears to have sat down and written his account during the voyage, for it was mailed to the *The Wide World Magazine* on 25 October, when he got to Sydney, and he received the pleasure of seeing it printed in the March 1901 issue[47].

For a start, it appears that the events took place on 15 August. When they arrived in port, a young fellow from the *Perth Morning Herald* had boarded, and asked: "Have you seen anything unusual this side of Leeuwin, Captain Thomson?"

"Why do you ask?" he replied, puzzled at how the news could have arrived before him.

"Oh, well, you see," said the reporter, "Captain Campbell, of the S.S. *Perth*, has just got in, and he reports having seen a sea-serpent off Rottnest Island, so I thought you might have seen it too. Of course, it all depends on what brand of whisky you use on board."

According to Captain Thomson, he then went over to the *Perth* to confer with his friend, Campbell, and they concluded that the *Perth* had seen the same monster twelve hours after the *Nemesis*, while the latter was in Vasse harbour. We must therefore assume that either Captain Thomson was laid over in Western Australia for two months, or he made two more return trips to Sydney, before deciding to break the news to the world. At any rate, here it is:

They were off Cape Naturaliste when he was called to the bridge by his third officer to observe something strange about half a mile [800 m] off, between them and the shore. At first he thought they were two whales, but as the distance shrank, it became clear it was "some enormous monster, longer than the *Nemesis* herself, and as flexible as a piece of rubber." Capt. Thomson provided the names of all the witnesses, including the passengers. The accompanying illustration, although drawn by an artist who was not a witness, appears to accurately follow his description. If you have ever flicked a rope and watched the waves move down the length, you will get an idea of what they saw. Essentially, it was a very long, thin creature which was progressing by great waves passing down its body, each arch extending so high out of the water that they could easily see the space underneath.

Fig. 3. The *Nemesis* sea serpent, as published in the *Wide World*. Note: this sketch was not made by the author, but by a magazine artist, based simply on the text.

It was greyish black in colour, and appeared to have no eyes. Indeed, from the semi-transparent nature of the skin and its oily appearance on the surface unlit by the sunshine, he gained the impression that the animal was "built of a soft, pulpy material" ie that it was an invertebrate, or animal without a backbone. Then, as it got closer, a remarkable display took place.

The creature had reared its head high above the waters, and was gently swaying it backwards, forwards, and round about, as if its body were composed of innumerable ball-joints. A huge fin or flap now shot out from behind the head, and circling in the air threw itself over the head and then back at right angles to the still vertical neck ! An instant later and it shaped itself into all sorts of fantastic forms, the under part being almost a pure white in colour.

Soon, however, the tentacle began to beat the waters and the head to move more violently.

As it came parallel to the ship, they were able to make a good estimate of its dimensions. The length of the *Nemesis* was 273 feet [83.2 metres], and the animal extended 20 feet, or 6 metres beyond it. They all agreed that its diameter was about 3 ft 6 in [107 cm], and since the arches came up just below the level of the foredeck, it was easy to establish that they were raised 16 feet, or almost 5 metres above the sea.

Eventually, as the monster sped off at an increasing speed, the captain set the ship to round Cape Naturaliste, and to dock at Vasse harbour, thereby allowing the *Perth* to see the creature and get into Fremantle ahead of them.

Since he claims to have compared notes closely with Captain Campbell, it is surprising that the latter confirmed that it was the same as the one he had encountered. The two were completely different. Also, although the description of *Perth*'s monster was not dissimilar to that of other sea serpent reports, Captain Thomson's account is a load of arrant nonsense. It is physically and biologically impossible. The moha moha was perfectly reasonable compared to this. It is beyond the laws of physics for a living tube just over a metre thick to lift itself into arches five metres above the water. Nothing with a backbone could flex its spine in such a manner, and it is hard to see how anything without a backbone could reach such a size or flex itself in such a manner, even without lifting itself so high out of the water. Also, such a thing has never been reported since. No, it is pretty certain that Captain Thomson was inspired to invent the story after hearing about his colleague's experience, and even then it took him two months to set the story in motion.

[20] According to the correspondent of the Melbourne *Age* at Yarram, something really dramatic happened just a few hundred metres off the east coast of Wilson's Promontory, Victoria late at night on Tuesday 14 May 1901[48].

YARRAM, Wednesday

The owner of the fishing smack, Sunbeam, Mr. W. B. M. Smith, reports having had an exciting adventure. At about midnight, when sailing between Rabbit Island and Miranda Bay, a huge sea monster attacked the boat, driving its teeth into the planks below the water line so fiercely that it broke them in its attempt to get at the occupants. Two of the teeth were extracted afterwards at the Welshpool pier, whilst the third was embedded too deeply in the timber to be withdrawn. The boat was travelling at a high rate of speed, or otherwise it might have been capsized, and as it was it was tossed onto its side. The crew describe the unknown monster as resembling a snake in appearance, with no fins of the back, which was out of the water. It lashed the sea into foam for a distance of 50 or 60 ft. [15 to 28 metres] from the boat, but being dark a good view of it could not be obtained.

Granted that it was too dark for a good view, don't you wish the journalist had asked a few questions and added a few more details? Like how big was the *Sunbeam*, and how many crew members were interviewed, what were the circumstances of the attack, and *what did the teeth look like*? After all, two of them had been collected, and one was still in the timber; you might think a reporter would be curious enough to ask to see them. Apart from anything else, it would confirm the story.

Despite the reference to a snakelike appearance and the absence of a fin, considering the darkness, I wonder if it were not some sort of fish, or even a seal, and the attack on the boat an attempt at self-defence. Later, you will read about another sea serpent which left its teeth in an oar.

I previously remarked that the stretch of Victorian coastline close to the New South Wales border has a history of sea serpent sightings. In the space of a week in July 1902 they were observed by two different ships in the same general area - and they may not have belonged to the same species.

[21] The first was the S.S. *Whangape*, which sailed from Devonport to Newcastle, and thence to New Zealand, where the

second officer, Mr Yeomans told his story. It was about 3 pm on July 6, and they were approximately seven miles [11¼ km] off the coast between the lighthouses of Cape Everard and Gabo Island. The weather was clear, with a moderate swell running. He was on the bridge when

> [h]e saw in the water, on the starboard side, about 80 yards from the steamer, a large snake-like creature swimming vigorously in a direction opposite to that in which the Whangape was proceeding. It appeared to be about 50 ft [15¼ m] long, and was black in colour, with a head resembling in size and shape that of a seal. It was furnished with large fin-like appendages, or flappers, of which there appeared to be two. Mr Yeomans watched it for a few moments while it pursued its way with undulating motion[49].

[22] It was also recorded that while they were at Newcastle, they heard that the same monster (?) had been observed by the crew of the S.S. *Chillagoe* in the same area. This is interesting, because it appears the *Chillagoe*'s captain, W. Firth had reported it on 13 July when it arrived in Sydney. The sighting must therefore have taken place a day or so before. In any case, the location was Ram Head, a small promontory a few kilometres east of Cape Everard. This one was said to be "a serpent of immense size", whose body did not show above the water, but whose length was estimated at 30 to 35 feet [9.1 - 10.7 m], with a seal-like head about two feet [60 cm] across. The ship changed course in order to inspect the monster, but when they were within about 100 metres (bearing in mind that a steamer, unlike a windjammer, is noisy), it raised its head out of the water, looked at the ship, and disappeared. What is particularly interesting, and which sets it apart from the *Whangape* specimen, was that it possessed four dorsal fins, each 4 to 5 feet [1.2 - 1.5 m] high and about 6 feet [1.8 m] apart[50]. Shortly beforehand there had been publicity of a sea serpent observed by the *Princess* in the south Atlantic, which possessed a double row of vertical, triangular fins, and the crew of the *Chillagoe* declared that the only difference was that the fins of their sea serpent were more angular.

[23] After that, things became very quiet along our coastlines - though not, I might add, as a result of diffidence on behalf of the national press, which was still happy to print the more dramatic (and questionable) reports from overseas. In April 1904, nevertheless, this mysterious paragraph appeared out of the blue in a local newspaper[51]:

> The sea serpent has been seen off Coal Cliff. If it is not the muchly-discussed serpent, we would like to know what it is. The monster is over 50 ft. [15 m] long with a most ungodly looking head.

With even the date and the name(s) of the witness(es) missing, this is not much to go on. I have attempted to find some more detailed report in some other newspaper, but in vain. Coalcliff is a small coastal town between Sydney and Wollongong.

[24] In July of the same year the second officer of the steamer *Yongala* told how, as they were on the way to Fremantle, he watched, not a sea serpent, but some sort of huge fish, disporting itself in the water. Apparently 20 feet [6 m] long, with a huge pair of fins, very much like wings, a dark brown upper body and white lower parts, it moved in a leisurely fashion, occasionally throwing portions of its body out of the water like a porpoise. As they approached Rottnest Island, a similar, but smaller fish was also observed.[52] The newspaper did not appear to have consulted any zoologist before rushing into print. In my opinion, they were obviously humpback whales, and their sizes underestimated.

[25] In January 1908 a new report came in from Norfolk Island, but this one was very strange.

> The sea serpent has turned up again, on this occasion at Norfolk Island. About 4 p.m. on the 12th ult. (writes our correspondent), a young son of Mr. Godfrey Christian was out on the cliff, when he saw what he supposed was a large rope drifting about. Upon informing his parents, they, with other members of the family, went to see what it was, and Mr. Christian pronounced it to be a sea serpent. It was carefully watched, as it was expected

it would come ashore on the beach, but was lost sight of after sunset. It was estimated to be over 500 ft. [150 metres] long, and about 2 ft. [60 cm] in diameter. The head was about 10 yds. From the beach, and the serpent appeared to be feeding. The head seemed very hairy, underneath bushy and long. It was of a grey color, intermixed with both dark and brown. Three pilot fish were seen, one on either side of the head, and one in front.[53]

The witnesses might have been close enough for a good look, but the length is impossible. Was it, perhaps, a misprint for "50 feet"? Even so, what could it possibly be, if the head was hairy, and no further identifying features were noted? Why weren't they more detailed in their description? Incidentally, the witnesses' surname indicates that they were descendants of Fletcher Christian, the leader of the Mutiny on the *Bounty*.

[26] To understand the events of October the following year, you must realize that the two locations frame the major southeast Queensland port of Bundaberg. Elliott Heads lays 21 km to the southeast, and Burnett Heads, with its lighthouse, 17 km northeast.

On Sunday 10th, Mr H. Harrison went fishing instead of going to church (a common practice, so it seems) and saw what he considered a "sea serpent of enormous proportions" three miles, or five kilometres out. I'm assuming, though the report doesn't say so, that he was in a boat at the time, but there was no indication as to how close he was to the animal.

First appeared the head like that of a conger eel, which was raised in the air and brought down with tremendous force, churning the water into foam; then appeared two large fins which resembled a small sail, the tail of somewhat similar appearance[54].

Its length being estimated at 60 feet [18 m], it was in sight for two hours, and travelling in a northerly direction. There were said to be many other witnesses to confirm the truth of the story.

A few days later, a letter came from Brisbane from a Mr George Collins, who had been on the steamer, *Musgrave* when it was approaching Burnett Heads the following Thursday[55].

Noticing a commotion a mile to the stern, they turned the ship around and came within 100 metres of a whale about 50 feet [15 metres] long, wallowing in the water, splashing it to a great height, and throwing up its great flukes, which were 10 to 12 feet [3 to 3.7 m] long. He suggested that Mr Harrison had seen the same thing. I'm afraid I have to agree with him. The description and behaviour is a pretty good match for a humpback whale in the middle of the seasonal migration - although they are normally heading south, rather than north, at that time of year.

[27] It was not until 1913 that the legendary monster again graced the Australian scene, but this time with a vengeance: two within three weeks. The first one occurred on 29 April[56], although it was not reported until the later one made news. It took place 12 miles, or 19 km, north of Point Hibbs, on the west coast of Tasmania, which means it must have been about the same distance south of the entrance to Macquarie Harbour.

The witnesses were Oscar Davis and W. Harris, employees of Hatwell Conder, the State Mining Engineer for Tasmania, who vouched for their reliability, and the fact that they were fully conversant with the seals and sea lions which frequented the coast.

They were walking along the coast just before sundown, when Davis noticed a dark object among the sand dunes about half a mile away. They approached to within 40 metres, when it suddenly rose and rushed down to the sea where, once it was about 30 metres out, it stopped, and turned around, displaying its small head and thick neck for about five seconds before submerging.

> "It was 15 feet [4.6 m] long. This measurement was checked by "stepping" the mark in the sand, where it had been lying. Davis has done much building and construction work, and knows what 15 ft. looks like. It had a very small head, only about the size of the head of a kangaroo dog. It had a thick arched neck passing gradually into the barrel of the body. It had no definite tail and no fins. It was furred, the coat in appearance resembling that of a horse of chestnut colour, well groomed and shining. It

was attractive in appearance, and in no way repulsive-looking. It had four distinct legs. It travelled by bounding, i.e., by arching its back and gathering up its body, so that the footprints of the fore feet came down level, and also, those of the hind feet. It made definite footprints; these showed circular impressions, with a diameter (measured) of nine inches [23 cm], and the marks of four claws, about seven inches [18 cm] long, extending outwards from the impression and away from the body. There was no evidence for or against webbing. The footprints showed about 4ft. [122 cm] between the marks of the fore and hind feet, and then a gap of about 10ft. [3 m], making a total "spring" of 14ft [4¼ m]. Laterally they were 2 ft. 6 in. [76 cm] apart. It travelled very fast; a kangaroo dog followed it hard in its course to the water, a distance of about [indecipherable] yds., and in that distance gained about 30ft [9 m]. When first disturbed it reared up and turned on its hind legs. Its height standing on the four legs would be from 3ft. 6in, to 4ft [107 - 122 cm].[57]

What can one say? Despite the rather unusual footprints, it was obviously some sort of sea lion, but which species? This time the press went to an expert, H. H. Scott, the Curator of the Victoria Museum. He opted for an out-of-place Weddell seal, *Leptonychotes weddellii*, because of its small head, which he suggested would be foreshortened, and thus appear even smaller, when it looked back at a witness. Now, the distribution of the Weddell seal hugs the borders of Antarctica, where it tends to spend much of its waking hours, and often its sleeping hours, under the ice. But a specimen was caught in robbing a fishing net off Encounter Bay, South Australia on 15 April 1913, just two weeks before this encounter, which was no doubt another reason why the zoologist nominated it as a possibility. However, there are many problems with this identification. For a start, although its head is small for a seal, it is still of the same order of magnitude. By no means does it approach that of a kangaroo dog. Its colour is not chestnut, but dark grey with white blotches. Also, its maximum length is 3 metres or 10 feet. Admittedly, witnesses frequently overestimate size, but in this case, they paced out the impression it made in the sand. Also, Weddell's seal is not a sea lion, but a true seal. Its hind limbs point backwards, and cannot be used in the method described. None of the other seals or sea lions around or near Australia fit the bill either.

Heuvelmans attached high importance to this sighting, because of his theory that the "long necked" sea serpent is a species of seal or sea lion. In his opinion, the animal which Davis and Harris encountered was a young member of the species, and confirmed his view that the said variety of sea serpent possesses no tail. I beg to differ. The theory will be discussed in more detail in the last chapter, but there was nothing in this report to indicate that the neck was long and thin. On the contrary, it was "thick and arched". All we can say is that this animal was a sea lion of an undetermined species.

[28] The second sighting of the year was made by the captain, the man at the wheel, the Marconi officer (ie wireless operator), and several saloon passengers of the S.S. *Dimboola* on 14 May. The *Dimboola* was a steamer plying the trade between the southern capitals. In early May it departed from Adelaide, and when it arrived in Fremantle, probably about 20th of the month, the skipper, William Millar dropped a bombshell. He announced what they had seen south of the Great Australian Bight[58]. Suddenly, it became hot news, spreading to every corner of the nation in both capital city and regional newspapers. Captain Millar was interviewed more than once, and provided both a written statement and two sketches. An internet search turned out 144 newspaper references. Ironically, the news appears to have never leaked out to the outside world, or to have been noted by any scholars. Until I rediscovered it, it had been completely forgotten.

It happened at 35° 30' S, 133° 40' E at 11.15 am. The weather was fine and the sea smooth, when a shout from some of the passengers caused the third officer, who was on watch, to look out at the starboard quarter. About a quarter of a mile (400 metres) away, the water was being disturbed by a shoal of porpoises approaching from the northwest. The attention was caught by the captain and the Marconi officer. I suspect the captain was exaggerating when he said there were thousands of them - though it has been known - but he claimed he had never seen such a huge number before. Among them were several young whales, "all blowing and having a good time". I am uncertain what species they belonged to, because the terms he used, "grampuses and blackfish", used to be attached to several different species. My best bet is Risso's dolphin (*Grampus griseus*) and false killer whales (*Pseudorca crassidens*) respectively, although "grampus" was also a term for a killer whale (*Orcinus orca*).

Although a quarter of a mile may sound a long way, they were watching them through nautical telescopes, which are designed to identify such things as flags at that distance. Suddenly, "this wonderful creature" rose up in the middle of them. Abruptly, the whole shoal changed course and headed north at speed, as if fleeing from the creature. I presume he estimated its length by reference to the whales. It was 50 feet, or 15 metres. He could see the head clearly, intermediate in size between that of a whale and a porpoise, alternately raised high out of the water and ducking into it, while its body, the colour of a brown seal, moved in a sinuous manner, occasionally showing a tail "of an exaggerated fish variety".

Presently, the whole ensemble disappeared, but not before both he and the Marconi operator were able to get some pencils and paper and make sketches, which he claimed matched each other closely. The sketches you see here were both made by the skipper, and you will immediately notice something not mentioned in the verbal description: something like a serrated fin on the neck, and possibly the fore part of the back. I wonder if this were the mane sometimes reported for the long necked sea serpent. It is commonly believed that sea serpents are elongated whales, and tail flukes, which I presume were horizontal, tends to confirm it.

When Captain had returned to Adelaide, he received in the mail a certificate granting him life membership in the "Fish Liars Association"[59], signed by President "Shovel Nose Shark" and

Honorary Secretary, "Cloud Crayfish". The captain laughed and said that, like most Scotsmen, he appreciated a joke, even on himself. (I thought Scotsmen were supposed to be "dour".) He did, however, add a few snippets of information: the head was visible 10 to 15 feet [3 to 4½ metres] above the surface, and it had "an appendage hanging from its chin like a goatee beard". You will notice that on the second sketch.

Fig. 4A. Illustration of the *Dimboola* sea serpent, as published in the *Sunday Times* of 25.5.1913, based on Captain Millar's original sketch.

Fig. 4B. Captain Millar's second sketch, as published in the *Daily Telegraph* of 31.5.1913.

Three attempts were made to explain it away. H. C. Dannevig, the Federal Fisheries Director said that did not believe in sea serpents, but if he had to hazard a guess at an identification, he would opt for a group of killer whales attacking a large whale[60]. This would produce a lot of churning of the water, and the heads of whales breaching into the air, along with the sinuous motion of porpoises following the action. Captain Millar replied that he had observed such fights, and this was nothing like one. (He also used the term, "killer" on this occasion, which makes me believe he had not used the word, "grampus" for the same species in his original report.)

Then, in mid-June, the steamship *Alcinous* was crossing the Bight in much the same area of the *Dimboola*, when they initially thought they saw the same animal[61]. With the aid of glasses, they were able to observe a great, sinuous object about 100 yards long. Alas! When it got closer, they saw that it was a shoal of seals, bobbing along in three parallel lines. It is notable, however, that there was no mention of a head rising and lowering in the front, or a fish-like tail in the rear. Also, it is unlikely that even a large shoal of seals would cause another shoal of porpoises and whales to change direction. Objects of this type have certainly been mistaken for sea serpents in the past, but it is unlikely it happened to the *Dimboola*.

Finally, David Stead, whom you will remember in the case of the giant shark in Chapter 1, came up with his own explanation: it was a giant squid![62] As we shall see, Mr Stead was to use the same argument in later sea serpent sightings, so it might be germane to discuss the issue here.

To such a degree has this monster captured our imagination that we are far more likely to encounter it in literature than in real life. Even those who have never read *Twenty Thousand Leagues Under the Sea* know of the submariners' battle with a school of giant squid (which have never been known to school). Peter Benchley followed up *Jaws* with *Beast*, about a giant squid 100 feet long (!), with habits more consistent with science fiction than science. Although it is octopuses which lurk in crevices on the bottom, while squid swim free in the open sea, the movie, *Reap the Wild Wind* had John Wayne as a diver fighting a giant squid in an undersea wreck. *Tarka the Otter* encountered a giant squid under the same circumstances in the book of that title. In *Biggles and the Deep Blue Sea*, the eponymous hero is attacked by a giant squid - in a lagoon! And in the most absurd scene in that absurd book, *Dr No* - sensibly omitted from the film - James Bond is dropped into an enclosure with a giant squid - as if you could just go out and collect such a monster of the deep for your aquarium! In *The Egyptian* by Mika Waltari, it was also the monster of the Cretan Labyrinth - another scene sensibly cut from the film.

The fact is, despite earlier legends, the species was not scientifically named until 1856, or seen alive until 1861. Then, in the 1870s, a large number of them were washed up, dead or dying, on the shores of Newfoundland, Labrador, and Nova Scotia. Without this habit of occasionally coming to the surface to die and be washed ashore, the giant squid might well be as legendary as the sea serpent.

The longest ever measured was 55 feet 2 inches [16.8 metres] long, but the body itself was only 5 ft 11 in. The biggest by far had the same length, but its body was said to have been approximately 20 feet [6.1 m] long. That's pretty big. However, a few reservations are in order. First of all, as explained earlier, most "cold blooded" animals continue to grow throughout life, and the giant squid is unusual in that it doesn't appear to have a typical adult size. In his book, *In Search of the Giant Squid*[63], Richard Ellis provided a list of specimens, mostly strandings, in an appendix. A length was included with 80 of these, allowing me to plot numbers against size[64]. It turned out that the numbers were more or less constant with all size categories except the largest, consistent with a species which grows at a constant rate throughout life, with the very big ones dropping off as they perish. The median size was 27 feet [8¼ metres], with 50 of the 80 being 30 feet [9.1 metres] or less. In other words, the vast majority of giant squids are going to be much smaller than the maximum.

But there is more to it than this. A squid has a spindle shaped body with eight arms, and two very long tentacles which are so long that, as a rule of thumb, they effectively double the length. However, all the above lengths are quoted inclusive of these two tentacles. Thus, a 10 metre squid, to use an example, would appear only 5 metres long when viewed on the surface. That is, if it could be viewed at a distance. They cannot undulate like a sea serpent, nor do they possess a "head" which can be raised above the surface, only a triangular tail which, if the squid were swimming backwards, which is quite common, would remain flat against the surface.

Not only that, but giant squid are denizens of the twilight depths, hundreds of feet down. They do not possess the largest eyes in the animal kingdom for nothing! Any one which appears on the surface is likely to be dead, or very, very sick. No, I think the giant squid is the least likely candidate for the sea serpent.

6. The Inter-War Years

During the First World War, 1914 - 18, Australians gave up seeing sea serpents or, more likely, gave up reporting them. Thus, an encounter in 1916 waited eighteen years to be reported, and then only as a response to publicity about the Loch Ness Monster. However, since it took place in the Top End, I shall defer it till Chapter 9. When a marginalised topic ceases to be mentioned, the process becomes self-fulfilling, as witnesses turn timid in coming forward.

[29] Nevertheless, the "drought" didn't long outlast the war. Take, for instance, this enigmatic report from February 1919:

> One night recently, after work time, two Kiama fishermen went out in a boat, and arriving at the ground, soon got to work. One hooked a big snapper and had him safely in the boat and was in the act of taking the fish off the hook when a huge and ungainly head belonging to some marine monster appeared and calmly annexed the fish from the hands of the scared fisherman. Startled at this sudden apparition both men, who had been looking at the fish, looked over the side of the boat, and lo, there was the serpent, fully twenty feet [6 m] of body showing, just making off. One of the men who has sailed on every sea in the world, says he never saw anything like the monster[65].

That's not much to go on. I suspect that fear and darkness caused an exaggeration of a more mundane encounter, for example, with a seal.

[30] Even more enigmatic was the story about the idyllic life of E. J. Banfield on a tropical island, which ended:

> Banfield is one of the few Australians who vows that he has seen a sea serpent. The reptile, which was about 60 feet [18 m] long, became stranded in shallow water off Dunk Island, but ere the naturalist could approach close enough to use his camera it managed to free itself and disappear[66].

Again, even less to go on! I have never previously heard of a sea serpent being stranded before. However, strandings are not unknown of the giant oarfish, *Regalecus glesne*, which have certainly contributed to the sea serpent legend. They are ribbon-like body fish of the middle depths, which never reach 18 metres, but are known to reach a third, and even half that length.

[31] By 1920, interest in sea serpents had dwindled, judging from the number of references in the press. Nevertheless, there did appear this brief paragraph of what happened off Beachport, South Australia in April[67].

> Our Mount Gambier correspondent writes: - A party of fishermen, whilst out snappering were alarmed by the sudden appearance near their boat of the head and sinuous neck of a fish or animal, which, from the casual glimpse obtained of it, was estimated to be about 12 ft. [3.6 metres] long. This strange monster raised its head, surveyed its surroundings, and then disappeared. The stranger was subsequently seen several times during the day. The imaginations of those who saw it stretched its length to 30 ft. It is declared to be a small sea serpent.

One gets almost frantic with frustration at the limited information these journalists seemed to think was appropriate. For example, did the creature stick its neck 12 feet out of the water, or does the measurement refer to both neck and body - in other words, does "12 ft. long" refer back to "head and sinuous neck" or "fish or animal"? Couldn't they even say what the head looked like? What was its colour? I would have been prepared to write this off as some sort of known species, except nothing known to science sticks a head and sinuous neck out of the water.

As for 1921, the only record was a letter to the editor of a Melbourne newspaper[68] in November by someone called "Interested", claiming that a sea serpent had recently appeared near Frankston recently, and a sportsman had fired some shots at it to no effect. Unfortunately, the sportsman failed to come forward to corroborate it.

[32] It says a lot about the atmosphere at the time that it was only when the mystery animal was in the news again six years later

that the witness came forth, and even then he chose to remain
anonymous.

At Green Island, about 13 miles [21 km] from Cairns, in the
winter of 1924, there rose from the sea part of the body of some
animal. It was only a few oars' lengths from the launch, and about
nine feet [2.7 m] of an arched neck was exposed. With a diameter
about 15 inches [40 cm], its color was a mottled brown and yellow.
The whole body must have been of great length. It was assuredly a
member of the serpent order, and not a porpoise, seal, dugong, or
tortoise, with all of which I am familiar. Others saw the animal. It
was no optical illusion, and there was no liquor on board.[69]

That last comment is typical when people report something
bizarre. (Nowadays, the use of drugs is also denied.) Of course, the
fact is, you have really, really drunk in order to have hallucinations
(DTs), and although alcohol may impair a person's ability to
interpret what he sees, witnesses know when they have been drunk,
and I am sure they do not talk about what they have seen while
under the influence.

[33] I confess to being baffled by the next report. It happened
at Sorrento, Victoria, on the Mornington Peninsula close to the
entrance of Port Phillip Bay, then, as now, a seaside holiday
destination. The date was most likely in the holiday period
Christmas 1924/New Year 1925, because in January 1929, a
Mr. J. R. Martin walked into the office of the Melbourne *Herald*
and told them that he had been reading their story about an
American expedition to find a sea serpent and he reckoned as knew
as much as any of them[70]. Four years previously, he claimed, he
had been walking on the beach at Sorrento when he saw, rolled up
on the sand and a similar colour to the sand, "a creature about 30
feet [9 m] long and as thick as a motor tyre". It was apparently
dead, but he was so fascinated by it, he kept watching until the tide
came in and washed it back. Then, much to his surprise, it began to
wriggle and disappeared behind some rocks.

If the creature were "rolled up" he may well have
overestimated the length, but I am still at a loss to know what it

was. There have been no plausible incidents of sea serpents being stranded on shore; their shape probably allows them to wriggle out of the shallows where a whale or dolphin would flounder. Alleged strandings have invariably been identified as something more mundane. As mentioned before, an oarfish is the most common candidate. However, it bears a dorsal fin right down the length of its spine which, at the front, turns into a vertical crest which is hard to overlook. More to the point, an oarfish is a *fish*. It can remain alive if stranded in very shallow water, but on land it will die.

[34] 1925 itself had scarcely begun when the Australian press was alive with the story of the encounter by the French ship, *Saint-François-Xavier* on the Noumea-Newcastle-Indochina route. One rural newspaper managed to obtain an extract from the official log from the agents, John Read and Company[71].

> At 6.30 p.m. on February 2, several officers, and a portion of the crew of the steamer St. Francis Xavier [*sic*] report having seen, when exactly abeam of the lighthouse at Port Stephens, a huge sea serpent of dark yellow color, about 60 feet [18 m] in length, and two feet [60 cm] in diameter.
>
> The steamer was about a mile [1.6 km] out from the shore, and passed within a few yards of the monster. While the vessel was passing it, the serpent appeared to be asleep, its head and tail formed five coils. On the centre of the back was a spike-like fin, resembling a shark's.
>
> Doubtless awakened by the noise of the propellers, it extended its head several yards out of the water, the head being turtle-shaped, with a graceful neck. It remained in this position for several minutes, and then disappeared.
>
> The Chinese members of the crew referred to the serpent as the dragon, a symbolic monster of Chinese mythology.

The paper reported that the lighthouse keeper had denied that either he or his staff had observed the monster. The ship's master was recorded as Captain Charlot in both the accounts, and in the simple shipping news in other journals. This is interesting, because on 18 March of that year, when the ship was in Haiphong harbour, the captain signed his name Raoul Jaillard in a private letter about the incident to his superior. Perhaps he was another officer, or perhaps the Australian press was in error, but it is worth citing the entire text, because it used slightly different wording, and came accompanied by a sketch. It was published twelve years later by Dr. P. Chevy, the Director of the Oceanographic Institute of Indochina[72].

> Sir, I am sending you a little sketch drawn at sea several minutes from the appearance of the famous sea-serpent. The second captain, the second lieutenant, the radio officer and the third engineer are unanimous in confirming the following lines:
>
> On 2 February 1925 while on passage from Nouméa to Newcastle, the ship making 10 knots [18½ k.p.h.], at 18.30 hours abeam of Port Stephens on the east coast of Australia, two masses like turtles' shells were seen floating 30 feet [9 m] from the ship on the starboard bow.
>
> Abeam of the engines there rose a big head like a camel's head, on a long flexible neck having a great similarity to a swan's neck. The height of the neck was about eight feet [2½ m]. The body, as thick as the big Bordeaux barrels, formed a chain of five loops; on the fourth loop, an aileron as on sharks of great dimensions, measuring 5 feet [1½ m] in height and in width at the base. The aileron seemed to be black in colour; the colour of the animal was dirty yellow, the skin smooth without appearance of scales.
>
> As it passed astern of the ship and was abeam of the starboard screw, the animal's head began to move backwards and forwards, which led us to think it had been touched by a blade of the screw; its movements seemed hindered and was not at all like that of the little snakes seen near the coast.
>
> The animal was visible *for fifteen minutes*, no optical illusion is possible. For, besides the testimony of the Europeans, the Blacks from New Caledonia serving as seamen on board, the Annamite boys and Chinese stokers all gave one cry: 'There's the Dragon!' The Chinese even made an offering to it.
>
> As night falls very quickly at that time we could not give other details, being one and all fairly taken aback by this fantastic apparition... [emphasis in original]

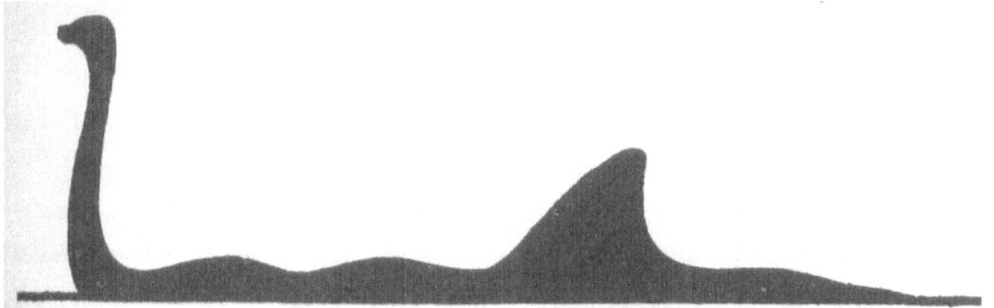

Fig. 5. Captain Jaillard's sketch of The *Saint François-Xavier* sea serpent.

From the sketch, it is clear that he regarded the head and neck as one of the loops. In any case, the colour and the presence of a fin make it very unusual, even by sea serpent standards.

[35] Something unusual, but quite different, appeared outside of Brisbane nearly six months later. On 23 July the Dutch ship, *Bawean* had just dropped off the Brisbane pilot and was setting out for Sydney when, according to Captain P. de Haan:

> We were suddenly aware of a violent disturbance in the water to starboard. A little later a long black body, estimated at 8 metres [26 ft] long, emerged at an angle of 45°, then fell back into the water with a loud splash, making the sort of waves we had already seen. It reappeared again, closer to us four times; the body, sticking out obliquely, which was about 1½ metres [5 ft] thick and was more or less cylindrical, seemed to have a long head, with a beak and eye, and rounded at the end. When the animal fell back, a fin about 4 metres [13 ft] long rose at an angle on the right side behind the head, and the body curved to this side when it fell. At the same time there rose out of the water, several feet away, a sort of tail, much thinner than the front part. On the top of the head the skin was black and pimpled, while underneath it was lighter and smooth. The erected 'fin' was much lighter still: almost white with black patches. Its breath was very clearly seen and heard. To my great regret nobody had a camera handy, and it was very difficult to focus glasses on the animal, as we did not know exactly where it would appear next. The shortest distance at which it appeared was about 350 metres[73].

This "fin" bothers me. Was it a fish-like fin, or a paddle, like that of a whale or turtle? The officer on watch thought it was an open jaw, but de Haan, who saw the animal head on could tell that it stuck out horizontally. That anything would possess a pectoral fin or flipper half the length of its body seems unlikely, and I suspect a typographic error. In any case, the beak and the visible breath suggest it was some sort of dolphin or, more likely, a ziphiid or beaked whale, many of which are known only from strandings or sightings.

[36] The report which arrived in August 1926 was brief to the point of uselessness.

> Charles Hillier and Percy Ross, while out in a boat between Bulli and Bellambi, were startled by the appearance of a sea serpent, which came alongside the boat. It measured fully 12 feet [3.6 m]. Its head was that of a snake, and the body like that of a porpoise. It twisted and turned in all directions, and was evidently spineless.[74]

Don't you just love the attention to detail by some journalists? There is no way from that account to determine whether it represented an unknown species, but my guess is that it was some variety of sea snake, albeit on the large side. (Bellambi is a site near Wollongong in New South Wales, and was to be the site of a genuine sea serpent visitation at a later date, as we shall see.)

[37] The details of the next sightings are not much better because, although it happened in 1926 or 1927, it was not until 1953 (!) that the witness, Alec J. Gracie wrote about it - in a private letter[75], and by that time he had mislaid his Norris Log-tables where he had noted the details. He had been the third mate on the *City of Manila* when it was crossing the Great Australian Bight on the passage from Melbourne to Fremantle (like the *Dimboola*, remember?). It was about six bells in the morning (7 a.m.), when he noted something about a mile away, looked at it through his binoculars, and handed them to the white quartermaster, who agreed it was unusual. It appeared to be six to eight arches,

which seemed to undulate, but it was in view for only about half a minute.

7. More and More of Them

The 1930s were born in the Depression and, although not everyone suspected it at the time, it was the last decade of peace. It was also a good period for sea serpents in Australia. The news of the Loch Ness monster in 1933, of course, strengthened the resolve of witnesses to come forth, and for journalists to take them seriously. Nevertheless, they didn't have to await the news from Scotland.

1930

[38] This was a very good year for sea serpents off the east coast. It began in June (a report dated Friday 13th said "last week") off Bellambi, N.S.W., which is about 7 km north of the centre of Wollongong, and has now been taken up by the Wollongong conurbium. Gay Richardson, with his three friends, Ron Wiley, James Gray, and Albert Lane got into Richardson's boat and went fishing about a mile [1.6 km] off the Bellami jettty, drifting through choppy water and reeling in the occasional snapper when, about half past two, they noticed what looked like wreckage about 80 metres away, and decided to get closer for a better look.

However, when they were within about 20 metres, suddenly a huge head and four feet [1.2 metres] of neck rose out of the water. Fins, fully three feet [90 cm] high projected from its shoulders. Its body was either brown or black, with a white belly. But what terrified them was that it had a beak like a pelican, and a mouth which, when opened, was big enough to swallow a man. Not surprisingly, they headed for the shore, with the monster not far behind them for about half a mile. They saw about 25 to 30 feet [7½ to 9 metres] of it, as it wriggled like a snake, and roared like a seal, only louder.[76] On the other hand, one of the witnesses was more specific about the length. He said he could not be sure of 25 feet, but he did see 8 to 10 feet of it, and it raised its head 6 feet in the air.[77]

David Stead, the fisheries expert (remember him?) was consulted, and this time made an identification which I think is spot on: it was a whale. In particular, he nominated the pike whale,[78] which is a type of rorqual. Rorquals should not be unfamiliar to the layman; the best known is the blue whale, the largest animal ever to have lived. The key feature of these whales is their wide, pleated mouth, which would certainly appear like that of a pelican when it sagged as the owner rose out of the water. No other "sea serpent" has ever been described with such a mouth, but it fits a rorqual perfectly. Furthermore, the colouring, beaklike head, the slender shape, and two short pectoral fins all match the description, as does the roar when under strong emotion. Thus, although Mr Wiley affirmed that they were familiar with whales off the coast, he had probably never observed one when it sounded ie raised its head in the air.

I believe what was then called a "pike whale" is today called the dwarf minke whale, *Balaenoptera acutorostrata*. However, I don't know if that was what Mr. Stead intended for, although he claimed it can reach 50 feet [15 metres], the dwarf minke is actually only half that size. The fin whale, *B. physalus* can reach 27 metres, and would also fit the bill, but there are several other species which could serve as contenders.

[39] While the Bellambi sea serpent appears to have been a false flag, so to speak, what turned up about 12 km to the north the following month seems to have been the genuine article, although the press provided minimal details. In the afternoon of Wednesday 2 July, Miss Amelia Bundle was on the cliffs of Scarborough when she saw it, and immediately called the postmaster, Mr W. Ferguson, and Mrs R. Ross, and together they saw the animal, estimated to be half a mile [800 metres] out to sea, slowly swimming southwards in the direction of Bellambi Reef. Constable Bleechmere arrived just after it disappeared, and suggested it might have been a school of porpoises swimming in line.

Mr. Ferguson was positive, however, that it was between 80 and 90 feet [24.4 and 27.4 metres] long. At intervals it would shoot up a long serpent-like neck and fearsome head, as though it were feeding[79].

Another newspaper said that a woman claimed it was dark greyish in colour[80].

It needs to be added that estimating distance and size at sea, without any frame of reference nearby, is pretty much hit and miss. All that can be said is that it was a good way off, and very big.

Two days later what was almost certainly the same creature appeared to the south, off Wollongong. This time, the witnesses were a local builder, Mr G. G. Heather, his son, Roy, and a friend, Mr Bert Tucker, who were at Heather's house at Cliff Road about one o'clock when a disturbance was noted about a quarter of a mile [400 metres] away[81]. But on this occasion, they had binoculars, and sufficient time to make observations.

"I was at lunch yesterday," [Mr Heather] told the "News" over the 'phone to-day, while a boy sat in the car outside the house facing the sea, at about 20 yards from the cliff edge. His attention was attracted by something he saw in the water, and when we turned the glasses onto it, I began to change my opinion regarding the previous reports of the presence of the thing. For a quarter of an hour I had a grandstand view, as it swam leisurely over a radius of quarter of a mile. I could see the undulations it formed moving through the water, but the head was not visible. It appeared to be between 50 and 60 feet [15 and 18 metres] long, and probably a foot [30 cm] thick. I could not see any fins, and the best description I could give its colour would be a dark shade. Then it showed that it could move very swiftly through the water. It disappeared, and a few minutes later, we picked it up again half a mile away, making out to sea."[82]

A fortnight later, the crew of the trawler, *David Blake*, spurred on by the previous news, also saw what they initially thought was a sea serpent off Wollongong. It appeared to be wriggling through the water, but when they got closer, it resolved into a barnacle covered log about 50 feet long with boughs protruding all around it. They were confident, therefore, in announcing they had solved the mystery of the Wollongong sea serpent[83]. Readers, however, may wish to compare its "wriggling" with the movement alleged by Mr. Heather and company.

[40] Be that as it may, the publicity encouraged one man, Captain C. R. Stuart to come forward and report what had happened six months before, when he was in charge of the trawler, *Bar-ea-mul* off Montague Island, which you will remember from 1893 [12]. He and the crew saw the monster only 20 yards from the trawler and, in fact, every time the nets were hauled up the monster was seen, at one time only six feet [1.8 metres] away. His descriptions is so remarkable, it deserves to be cited verbatim.[84]

> "The front part resembled a huge shamrock, with what looked like the middle leaf much bigger than the others," he said. "The head, which seemed like a leaf, had a huge mouth and eyes the size of a saucer, which glowed dully. Two fins on each side of the head were not quite as big as the middle one, and seemed to be used as an aid in propelling he monster through the water. This huge head, with fins on either side, was at least 16ft. [4.9 metres] across, and was covered with a scaly substance. From the head there was at least 20 feet [6 m] of scaly monster above the water, besides what was below. The body was a slate grey color, and the head black. About 10ft. [3 m] down the body was a small dorsal fin, very much like that of a shark, but which seemed absurdly small, considering the bulk of the body."

My initial response in reading this story was to label it a hoax: fun and games on the part of a seaman in the wake of sea serpent tales in the press. But on second thought, the identification became obvious. Allowing for some exaggeration and misinterpretation induced by the shock of the encounter, it is a reasonable description of a humpback whale, *Megaptera novaeangliae*. True to its generic name (*Megaptera* means "big wing"), the humpback's pectoral flippers are about a third as long as the body, and set back about a similar distance from the front, so the head and flippers really would resemble a shamrock. Although the head is nowhere near 16 feet across, it is huge, as is the mouth, and there really is an absurdly small dorsal fin. As for the "scales", these would have been clusters of barnacles over the whale's body, especially the head. In fact, its skin actually provides rough patches for the barnacles to attach to.

[41] Although the crew and passengers of the Dutch Ship, *Nieuw Zeeland* claimed that they did not "subscribe to the sea-serpent theory", it was certainly on their collective mind when they arrived at Brisbane and reported what they had seen south of the border, as they were approaching Cape Byron on the afternoon of Thursday 24 July.

> The creature had a head like a crocodile, was longer than a whale, and spouted two jets of water high into the air. The noise made by the fearsome thing resembled that of a bellowing cow. The swishing of the tail caused a great commotion in the water, resembling that caused by the propellers of a vessel.[85]

You will note how the journalist carefully avoided any questions which may have clarified the animal's identity, such as: the state of waves, the distance, the duration of the sighting, how long they believed a whale to be, and whether a "head like a crocodile" meant that it had opened its mouth to reveal teeth, or just that the head was long and slim. The visible spouting proves it was some sort of whale. As we shall see in the last chapter, many people believe sea serpents to be prehistoric whales, but we needn't go down that track, for there are many known species as contenders. The obvious choice would be the uncommon fin whale: 27 metres long, streamlined, with a long, triangular head, and a spout up to 6 metres high. Even the "bellowing" is consistent with the low pitched male mating call.

But that was in northern New South Wales. Getting back to the South Coast sea serpent, fisheries expert, David Stead identified it as either a giant squid, a whale shark, or a basking shark, and that the submarine net between the Jervis Bay heads would catch it[86]. Well, it didn't!

[42] Jervis Bay, with its naval base, is a more or less circular bay south of Wollongong. Huskisson is a village almost exactly opposite the narrow entrance. On Sunday 3 August,

Mr. J. Johnston, managing director of Johnston's Musical Instruments Ltd., and his employee, Mr. J. J. McCullogh were returning from a business trip, and called in at Huskisson about 10.30 in the morning. At 10.35 Mr Johnston noticed something about a quarter of a mile [400 metre] out in the bay which he first took for a long boat crowded with people, but they soon realised it was alive.[87]

At the distance involved, one must have reservations about the precise dimensions they cited, but it was essentially a "long, undulating thing" 30 to 35 feet [say 10 metres] long, consisting of four humps, with a series of regular spikes or fins 3 feet [90 cm] high. At one point they saw a head, 3 feet long and shaped like an alligator's, appear a few feet above the water. Sometimes it would submerge for a few minutes before reappearing. It appeared black, but that may have been because the sun was behind it. The fact that the four humps were always in line for the 23 minutes they watched it indicated that it could not have been a group of porpoises (or a giant squid or shark!). At a speed much greater than any current, it travelled about a mile [1.6 km] across the bay, turned around, swam towards the mouth of the bay, then did another about turn and retraced its path, before rounding the reef in the middle of the bay and disappearing out to sea. So much for the anti-submarine net! Both the witnesses independently made sketches of the object, but no newspaper appears to have published them. It is also reported that they took a couple of snapshots, but the distance was too great to reveal anything but a tiny speck.[88]

I might add that one newspaper[89] stated that a monster called "Bellambi" had been present in Jervis Bay 35 years before, but I can find no record of it.

[43] But sea serpent mania was still in full swing on 8 August, when an excited group of citizens espied what they imagined was a sea serpent in Newcastle Harbour, which turned out to be a very big, very old, and very sick whale[90]. However, two days later something more mysterious turned up off Southport, in the Queensland Gold Coast[91]. About 8 o'clock in the morning a

Brisbane man, Mr J. Jackson, was watching a steamer in the distance with field glasses, when he saw something he took for a spouting whale close to the bar. Suddenly, a head "like that of a monster turtle" was raised 10 to 12 feet [3 to 3.6 m] out of the water, in a line of breakers about 25 yards from the bar. He had no trouble observing it with the binoculars, and the children watched it with the naked eye. It disappeared, but once again raised a portion of its body, which was as thick as a man's.

[44] But this was nothing compared to what allegedly raised its vast bulk in front of four startled fishermen just off Port Kembla, N.S.W. on Sunday 7 September. Their names were Charles Sloan, T. Mulligan. C. Dicks, and a Russian without a name. I shall let Mr Sloan describe it[92].

> "We were in a 20-foot [6 m] launch, drifting in a north-east breeze, about 11.30," he said. "About 30 feet [9 m] away we saw the monster just about to submerge. About 100 feet [30m] of its back was exposed. There were five or six spikes along its back, the three near to the head being about two feet [60 cm] long. The tail seemed to have a spread of about 20 feet. The serpent was about 10 or 12 feet [3 to 3.6 m] across the back, the body being a dirty grey. The head was very much like that of an elephant. When it submerged the surface of the water was left smooth and oily."

Were it not for the "five or six spikes", I would say they had got up close and personal with a blue whale, the largest animal which has ever lived, but it has only a single, short dorsal fin set far back. I cannot think of any other whale which would fit the bill, even if the size were exaggerated, and "sea serpents" are not normally described as so thick. On balance, I think this represents a mixed up description of a known whale rather than an unknown species.

[45] The final sighting of the year took place off Narrabeen, now the northernmost suburb of Sydney, right in front of the house of Reginald G. Parrington in Ocean Street. It was 6.30 a.m. on Tuesday 18 November ie probably just before sunrise.

Mr Parrington used to sleep on the verandah, and at first he thought it was the mast of a ship, until it crashed into the water with a splash. Thinking a ship had capsized, he called his wife and his son, Harry and got out his field glasses. The object was about three quarters of a mile, or 1.2 km away - again the vague estimate of the distance, followed by a vague estimate of size. It appeared to be 50 or 60 feet [15 or 18 m] long, and what he had initially taken for a mast was its tail (!), sticking 20 feet [6 m] out of the water and splashing water 30 feet into the air.

> The body was moving like a snake, and the huge head had a big fin where it joined the neck. The body was dark. It might have been green, or grey, but owing to the distance I could not tell the exact color.[93]

He was adamant that it was not a whale, for the tail came to a point. His wife and son rushed to the beach and saw it head south towards Long Reef and disappear. Even five year old Joan Priddle from next door saw it, but when she called her parents, they assumed it was a school of porpoises and ignored her. This is the first time I have ever heard of a sea serpent waving its tail high in the air, but Mr. Parrington thought it was important enough to phone the South Head Signal Station and report it.

Thus, 1930 was a busy year, with a lot of people unable to tell a whale from a sea serpent but, nevertheless, a number of genuine unidentified sea creatures putting in an appearance.

1931

[46] Tabourie Lake is a small village on the south coast of New South Wales at approximately 35½° south latitude. One day in the beginning of February 1931, or perhaps on the last day of January, Walter Roots was taking a holiday from his home in Goulburn and fishing off the rocks, when a frightening monster swam just beneath him.

> "It was reddish brown in colour, and was from 25 to 30 feet [7½ to 9 metres] long, the head resembled that of a pig, and behind the head were what looked like two floppy arms. The body suggested

a huge barrel, and the tail was vertical. The eyes were protruding, and were the size of saucers, while the teeth were sabre-like, and at least six inches [15 cm] long. The animal rose at one time with a fish in its jaws, the front part of the body, coming about 5 ft. [1½ m] from the water. The animal was grunting like a pig. After biting the fish in two, it chewed one portion, and then dived and brought the other portion to the surface.[94]

The monster was obviously a seal or sea lion, the "vertical" tail being its hind flippers held at that angle. But what kind, since it was twice the size of the biggest species? So when Paul Cropper sent me that clipping, I interpreted as an unknown giant species, and published it accordingly. However, seals and sea lions have to come onto land to breed, so I have come around to Paul's suggestion that it was a leopard seal, *Hydrurga leptonyx*, its size exaggerated by Mr Roots' terror. Even so, a leopard seal is dark grey above and paler below, but who knows how it would appear in water during a brief encounter? There are other seals and sea lions of a brown colour, but they are smaller.

Tabourie Lake is not far from Bateman's Bay. On Friday 17 July, G. Patrech and Bill Lawler were fishing there at the mouth of the Clyde River when a "sea serpent" broke the surface eight feet [2½ metres] from their boat, dived, and reappeared three more times. It was brown, about 12 feet [3.6 metres] long, 2½ feet [75 cm] thick, with a flat head and white jowls.[95] 12 feet would be par for the course for a leopard seal. A couple of weeks later, a female leopard seal was, in fact, washed ashore at Bateman's Bay, and taken to the Coogee Aquarium. She was recorded as 15 feet long, which the report admitted was oversized for her species, and the opinion was expressed that she had deceived many into thinking they had seen a sea serpent[96]. Mystery solved!

1932

[47] In 1933 Norman Caldwell was taken on a shark fishing holiday in the Great Barrier Reef by professional shark hunter, Boyd Lee, and later wrote about it in a book entitled, *Fangs of the Sea*.[97] At one point Caldwell was working on shore while Lee was

at sea, and when the latter arrived, he announced that he had seen a sea serpent the previous evening at dusk. Caldwell lightheartedly asked him for details, and then provided the explanation: a huge shark had smashed through a net, and Boyd agreed that what he had seen could easily have been the shark with the broken net trailing from its head.

That episode would, by itself, be inconsequential. I mention it only to demonstrate that Lee was genuine in his belief about sea serpents. The significance of this is that, later, they were located at a reef 27 km northeast of Hayman Island, and he announced that this was the spot where a sea serpent had been encountered eight months before ie in 1932. He and a companion were anchored close to the reef when an enormous turtle - at least four foot [1.2 metres] long and estimated to weigh 500 pounds [227 kg], plainly looking for something, or expecting something to happen. Lee stood on the mast, and his companion sat on the cabin roof, and watched it.

> Before the turtle had time to know what had happened, a mighty head, a head that resembled the head of a giant snake, came out of the water, and struck once, only once, at the turtle. Then the turtle and the vast sinister head that had engulfed it, disappeared. I repeat, that turtle must have weighed over five hundred pounds ...

Needless to say, he and his companion took off for their lives.

Caldwell believed his friend. He said that Lee was not above a leg-pull, but not about fishing. It was too important in his life for him to spin wild fish stories. Maybe. However, I need to point out that nothing of that size and voraciousness has ever been reported elsewhere. Furthermore, he mentioned a snakelike head, something which is hardly ever reported in plausible cases, but typical of made-up stories, because people automatically assume that a "sea serpent" must be a genuine serpent.

8. The Year of the Sea Serpents and the Last Dragons of Peacetime

Sea serpents appear to have taken an holiday from Australia in 1933, but they were back with a vengeance in 1934, even more so than in 1930. It could well be entitled, "The Year of the Sea Serpent", because eleven of them turned up in various guises all up and down the east coast.[98]

[48] The first made its appearance on 31st January in front of eight people, including some still in the water, at Ocean Grove, a seaside resort not far from Geelong, Victoria, at a distance of about a quarter of a mile [400 m]. The owner of a local guest house had a good look at it, and stated that it was long and sinuous, as sea serpents are supposed to be, black on top and white underneath. He does not appear to have been able to describe the head, but it dived several times, and the two dorsal fins, three or four feet [90 or 120 cm] high were clearly visible. Interestingly, he failed to describe the shape of the fins.[99] Were it not for the double fin, I would identify it as a killer whale. As it is, I am not prepared to rule out some mundane explanation.

[49] The next encounter allegedly took place at Anglesea, a short way southwest from Ocean Grove, on the weekend of 17/18 February, and is very weird.

When emptying crayfish pots off Anglesea fishermen found that the ropes of three were entangled round a huge fish. They described it as being about 9ft [2.74 m] in length, with a 6in [15 cm] neck, and a head measuring about 15in [38 cm] in length and 10in [25 cm] in breadth. There were two fins or flippers near the head, each measuring about 3ft 6in [107 cm] by 1ft 6in [46 cm]. The body, which was of a dirty black colour, was 4ft [1.2 m] across and about 2ft 6in [76 cm] in depth. There were five distinct spines showing down the back. One of the fishermen struck several blows on the monster's head with the tiller, but the timber bounced off without making an impression. The monster then slipped from the ropes and disappeared.[100]

This, may I humbly suggest, is a pretty poor specimen of journalism. We are not told how many fishermen were involved (?three), and I am willing to be bet they weren't questioned separately. In fact, I doubt if they were questioned at all. It should be obvious that the animal was not measured while alive, and the measurement estimates in feet and half feet confirm it. I am therefore suspicious of the estimates of 10 inches and 15 inches. This is not how people normally estimate size by eye. Also, I would have thought that any witness of basic education can distinguish between a fin (a fine membrane stretched between thin rays) and a flipper (solid flesh around a bony frame). Nor are we told whether the fin or flipper was attached to the body by its long or its short axis. Were there any scales or tail fin? The "five distinct spines" suggests a fin but, although I am no ichthyologist, and am aware that there are a lot of bizarre-looking fish out there, I find it difficult to imagine a fish with a neck and a swollen body. On balance, I think this was a hoax.

[50] On a Wednesday in March - either 1st or 8th - the Tetley brothers were walking down to the sawmill in Ulladulla, on the south coast of New South Wales, when they saw what they initially thought was the limb of a tree sticking out of the water just off the pier. But then it raised itself at least six feet [183 cm] out of the water, and they saw it was something like a dog's head waving around like a snake, but before they could get close, it disappeared.[101]

That is not much to go on, but the things which started popping up in North Queensland in the second half of the year were mostly better described, and they were a disparate collection.

[51] On 3 August film-maker, Robert Steele returned from north Queensland, where he had been engaged in making documentaries[102], so his encounter probably took place in July. However, he didn't report it until 14 August, when news of the

Mourilyan Harbour sighting (see [53]) made the morning newspaper. It happened when he and his co-director, Pierce Mack were returning from Orpheus Island, an elongated island due east of Ingham. A serpentine creature came up close to the boat and effortless followed them for a quarter of a mile, its head mostly level with the surface, but occasionally raised three or four feet above. In accordance with Murphy's law, their cameras were in another boat, but at least Mr Steele provided a sketch. He described it as:

> Twenty-five feet [7.6 metres] long, a snake-like head with fins on either side, very small eyes, a tail more like an eel than a snake, the body about 12 inches [30 cm] in diameter, no particular fangs or tongue showing, and the body an impressive lime green tinged with brown about the fins.[103]

Fig. 6. Orpheus Island sea serpent

This is one of those very strange stories made even stranger by the fact that it does not match any other strange story. On the coasts opposite, there does exist a lime green python, *Morela viridis*, popularly, and appropriately called the green tree python. However, apart from the fact that it would be out of place in the sea, its maximum length is 2.2 metres, and it lacks both fins and an eel-like tail. The last two features would suggest some unknown species of outsized eel.

[52] The next event happened in the first week of August, when the fishing vessel, *Rahata* was anchored off North Reef, a tiny reef in the Capricorn Group 120 km from Yeppoon, noted mostly for its lighthouse. It was about midday, the sea was dead calm, when Mr. H. Mills was making dumplings for a stew when a twelve year old lad cried out, "Look at that great snake!" Mr Mills turned, to see, about ten metres away, two great curves of a mighty animal, each about 10 feet [3 metres] long, practically as round as 40 gallon drums, brownish green in colour, with scales as big as his hand. He called to his shipmates, but before they could arrive on deck, it had disappeared, leaving a great swirl in the water.[104]

[53] The encounter at Mourilyan Harbour was actually the first of this mid-year series to be reported, and it encouraged the others to come forward. Mourilyan Harbour is not far south of the larger town of Innisfail. Late on Saturday night, 11th August a group of business people from Innisfail set out on a fishing expedition. Their names were W. Chung, E. How Kee, B. Clark, P. Ogden, and R. Kimlin, and about dawn they reached a point about 3½ miles [5.7 km] from Mouilyan Harbour called "The Deep Hole". The sea was as smooth as glass.

Suddenly, a snakelike head, armed with protruding teeth, emerged several feet out of the water about 30 yards from their launch, and gazed at them with its small eyes. Behind the head they could easily see a turtle-like back 8 feet [2½ metres] wide and 40 or 50 feet [12 or 15 metres] long, marked with what looked like the scars of old wounds. The tail appeared serrated and covered with large spikes. It began to swim slowly away, but when about 100 yards distance, submerged, only to resurface three minutes later much closer, and approached to within 30 feet [9 metres], when it began swimming around in circles emitting a half-gasping, half-whistling sound. Then it remained motionless for about 20 minutes, before it moved seaward, following the channel, and after 15 minutes it had disappeared.[105]

It is easy enough to read something like this, roll your eyes, and pass over it, but stop and think. Did these five people just decide to make up such as story and, if so, for what purpose? Potentially making yourself a laughing stock is not a good way to gain your 15 minutes of fame, especially if you're a businessman. Remember: this was the initial story which started it off. It is not as if they were inspired by a lot of earlier stories to have a bit of fun with the press.

[54] The sighting exactly seven days later further south, off Townsville, was reported in special detail because one of the witnesses, Oscar Swanson not only alerted the press, he also wrote to a marine biologist, A. H. E. Mattingley, who published it in the *Victorian Naturalist*.[106]

The witnesses were Oscar Swanson, William Quinn, and Swanson's nine-year-old son, Harold, who set out in a 14 ft [4¼ m] motor launch in the morning of Sunday 19 August, intending to fish near the Fairway Beacon, at the end of the Platypus Channel, about 6 km from Townsville. The sea was as smooth as glass. Having seen four whales the previous day, Swanson was eager for his son to have the same experience, and told him to be on the lookout. To their surprise, he pointed out four stationary objects in a line about three quarters of a mile [1.2 km] beyond the beacon. It was not a whale, but some sort of sea monster as big as a whale, which they were able to approach to within about 150 yards. The creature was motionless, but then, perhaps disturbed by the noise of the launch, it submerged. It did not dive, but simply sank slowly like a submarine. Fearing it might come at them, they headed back, and after five minutes, it rose again at the same place, just like a submarine. By then they were at the beacon, and were able to climb its ladder to watch it carefully, but it did nothing except sway its head, so after about half an hour they decided to return with a camera.

Upon reaching the wharf, Swanson phoned Jim Gibbard, the sub-editor of the *Townsville Bulletin*, who arrived with press photographer, Mr Ellis, and two cameras. So, leaving the boy behind, the four of them set off, only to see the S.S. *Marella* approaching the site where the monster had been, and they suspect the sound of its engines scared it away. However, Mr Ellis did see two dark objects, 20 feet apart deep down, which might have been the animal.

Fig. 7. Swanson's sketch of the Townsville sea serpent.

Figure 7 is Swanson's sketch of what it looked like although, from his description, the head ought to be longer. The head was held about 8 feet [2½ metres] out of the water, and was also 8 feet long, resembling that of a turtle in shape, with the mouth closed and the eye small. The whole animal was greenish grey in colour, with "three curved humps about 20 feet [6 m] apart, and each one rose from 6 feet [1.8 m] in the front to a little less at the rear". Judging from the sketch, 20 feet probably means from the top of each hump to the other, making the total animal 60 feet, or 18 metres long, not including any tail. However, if he meant that the empty space between the humps was 20 feet, then it would have been very big indeed.

He added that the whole body was covered with scales, which appeared to be butted and perpendicular, and the size of saucers. Also on the body were what he assumed to be barnacles, some as large as soup plates but since, as Heuvelmans pointed out, barnacles are seldom more than 5 cm in diameter, they were more likely to be some sort of natural growth or protuberances. Heuvelmans also noted that the impression of vertically overlapping scales is probably due to Swanson's lack of artistic skill.

The mystery animal apparently put in two other appearances that same day, because the following day the same newspaper carried the following story[107]:

The fishermen who saw the sea monster near the Fairway Beacon at midday on Sunday were not the only persons to sight it that day. At a quarter to seven in the morning a party aboard a yacht sighted it between Cockle and Bolger's Bay just off Magnetic Island. It lifted its tail out of the water several times and dropped it . The tail was not the fluke tail of a whale, but more that of a huge eel. On the third occasion when the sea monster was seen it was by some men engaged in fishing just outside the eastern breakwater. That was about 3.30 in the afternoon.

Magnetic Island is, of course, just a couple of kilometres from the sighting by Swanson's party. I wonder whether a tail like an eel means it had a long, thin fin, or simply that it was long and pointed, I suspect the latter.

Townsville is somewhat over 200 km by sea from Mourilyan Harbour. An animal the size of a whale could easily reach it in seven days. Nevertheless, both "monsters" were described in detail, and it seems impossible to reconcile them. The Orpheus Island creature, of course, was even more different. If the witnesses were trustworthy, then we are left with the remarkable conclusion that three separate species were involved. On the other hand, the meagre details of the North Reef animal might be referable to the one seen at Townsville.

[55] Four days later, it was Bowen's turn - or at least, Bowen was the nearest town. It sits on a peninsula at one end of Edgecumbe Bay, with Cape Gloucester at the opposite end, about 24 km away. To the north of the cape is Gloucester Passage, to the south, Sinclair Bay. Well, it was between these two sites at about 10.30 on the morning of Wednesday 23 August, a well-known local fisherman called Mr. H. Hurst, happened to see something large about 200 yards away heading in the direction of Sinclair Bay. The sea was dead calm at the time, and he was accompanied by two others, C. Hurst and J. Ayles. At first they thought it was a whale, but when it raised its head 8 feet [2½ metres] out of the water, they halted.

It appeared to be about 30 feet [9 m] in length. It had a head like a large turtle, and a body like a huge armoured hose.[108]

That meagre description would be consistent with the Townsville monster. It certainly didn't look like anything they might want to deal with, so they headed off to Bowen.

[56] On Thursday 30 August, the motor ship, *Trentbank* left Townsville for Montreal with a load of sugar. The following day, at 2.31 pm its master, Captain Porter send a wireless message to Messrs Howard Smith Ltd. (a shipping company): "Sighted monster off Penrith Island".[109] That is all we know about the sighting. One presumes Captain Porter could recognize a whale, but who knows? Penrith Island is a little island with a lighthouse 60 km off Mackay.

[57] On Wednesday 12th September, it was the turn of Coffs Harbour, in northern New South Wales.[110] Two deep-sea fishermen, Charles Blanch and Alfred Jackson saw what they thought was a log four miles [6½ km] from the entrance of the harbour, but only to realise it was some sort of animal 40 feet [12 metres] long. Not only that, but it had two legs, each a foot [30 cm] thick, 20 feet apart. Suddenly, as they got closer, it rolled over, and a head appeared, which both of them described as like a horse's. Then it gave a snort and plunged into the depths, raising a cloud of spray.

This does not sound like any of the other sea serpents. The newspaper consulted the fisheries scientist, Mr Stead again. He said it was a giant squid!

[58] It was back to Queensland for the last sea serpent visitation of 1934, this time at the mouth of the Burnett River, downstream from the major city of Bundaberg. To be precise, it was close to the locality of Round Hill, just to the north of the mouth, and not to be confused with the town of that name much further north. The Brisbane *Telegraph* stated that it had been sighted there several times, but provided details only of the last one, on Sunday 7th October.[111] On that day the passengers of a fishing launch watched it swim around in large circles at high speed, sometimes so close to the shore they thought it might beach itself. After twenty minutes it headed off to sea and was lost to sight. The newspaper claimed it was similar in size and shape to the creature seen in Mourilyan Harbour by Mr Chung's party, but the only specific details provided were to say that:

> It had a peculiarly-shaped head on the end of a long and thin neck, which at intervals was raised above the water in a sideways sweeping motion,

[59] Such was the last for a record year. In 1935 the action moved to Victoria. In the middle of June two lads were strolling along the beach near Blacknose Point, which is very close to the southern extremity of Portland Bay, when they saw what they first thought was a school of porpoises. However, when it came closer they realised their mistake, and moved to higher ground because, as they said, they did not know whether it had legs.

> The body, it is reported, was a slaty blue color, from 80ft. to 100ft. [24 to 30 metres] long, with a neck between 15ft. and 20ft. [4½ to 6 metres] long, the head being something the shape of a giraffe's. The head was high in the air, the body had a dorsal fin and a wide tail, something like that of a whale, with serrations on the end, and slaty grey stripes along it.[112]

They noted that great masses of spray were thrown up as the tail thumped the water. The animal was travelling parallel to the shore, but then turned and headed off to sea, the head and neck being visible, so it was said, for several miles.

[60] Barwon Heads is just a short distance from Ocean Grove, which you will remember from the beginning of this chapter, and not far from Port Lonsdale and Queenscliff. On 29 July 1935 two unusual events took place in this general region.

The first occurred when some road workers, about a mile from Barwon Heads, looked over a cliff and saw something that they initially thought to be a whale, seal, or sea lion on the beach, but then decided it didn't look like any of them. What a good idea, they thought, if they could capture it alive and put it on display!

The foreman sent off some of the men for a draught horse and some rope. Alas! When they tried to lasso it, it waddled off into the water. It was covered in fur, and described as

[a]bout 15 ft. [4.6 metres] long, greyish color, snake-like head, with an enormous mouth, white stripes under the chin.[113]

I have not the slightest doubt that this was a seal or sea lion.

[61] The second encounter was more dramatic. Two fishermen were sailing a few kilometres off Port Lonsdale when a monster appeared just three metres away from their boat, its head poised in an attitude suggesting an "imminent swoop". One of them picked up a gun and shot it. The creature disappeared, only to reappear as belligerent as even. The fisherman's second shot was a misfire, but the third one went home, and the animal decamped. It was described as:

20 ft [6 metres] long and 8 ft [2½ metres] thick, with a head four times the size of a diver's helmet, eyes like saucers, a neck 3 ft [90 cm] long and like a snake's, and a coat of short, black fur.[114]

Elsewhere, they were identified as Arthur and Herbert Hoppen, and Melbourne scientists cautiously identified the monster as a leopard seal.[115] That sounded quite reasonable to me or, if it wasn't a leopard seal, then some other, larger seal. However, in 2018 I was contacted by Arthur Hoppen's grandson, who insisted his grandfather had always insisted the identification was false, and he kindly provided me with the story as his ancestor related it to him. It says a lot for the current attitude towards sea serpents that he has requested his name not be mentioned.[116]

In 1980, I asked my grandfather, A Hoppen, about the time when he saw the sea serpent down near Point Lonsdale.
At the time of the sighting in 1935, A Hoppen was 21 and H Hoppen was 26.
He didn't like to talk about the sighting as they were criticised and ridiculed at the time. I remember the story very clearly.
On the day of the sighting they were returning from a fishing trip in a trawler and about to make their way in through The Rip,

which is the treacherous entrance to Port Phillip. They had just passed the Lonsdale Reef and were turning into the channel, just putting along, probably at about 5 knots. The weather was fine and the water slightly choppy but not rough.

He indicated the creature came up out of the water about 10-20 yards off the starboard side and moved closer to the stern of the trawler within a minute or so. He was standing on deck and its head was level with his, putting the head of the creature 6-8 feet out of the water. He said it had a big head and gestured with his hands what looked like a couple of feet in diameter. The head was sort of round and it had big black eyes.

He described the eyes as jet black and pointed to a saucer on the coffee table and said "a bit bigger than the little plate here" and indicated with his hands about 6-8 inches diameter, I think he even said at least 6 inches [15 cm]. He then stopped for a few seconds recounting the memory, sat back on the couch and said it was intelligent and was looking straight at them. I recall that he shook his head a little bit and said it was quite frightening knowing it was focused on them.

Being young and inquisitive, I asked for more detail.

The head was completely black and there was a slight rim around the eyes, also black but maybe slightly lighter around the rim of the eyes. It did not blink. He mentioned the eyes were convex just like a big fish.

I then asked him for more detail about the head and eventually we got it down to being a round shape looking at it from the front and more oval on the side view. The mouth was a slit that came around the side of the head a bit and remained closed so he didn't know if it had teeth or not. He didn't recall nostrils or any other feature but said it probably did but in the heat of the moment he didn't study it that hard for details.

The neck was long and thinner than the head and gestured with his hands which looked like about 1-foot diameter. He made that classic gesture with his arm and hand that people associate with a snake about to strike, simulating the creature coming out of the water. The neck was thicker down near the water line. As it moved, keeping up with the trawler, the head stayed in one position and the neck seemed to move in a forward motion as if it was swimming along with them. Lower down the neck it had a few greyish round markings, sort of what sounded to me like a mottled appearance.

It was smooth and didn't seem to have any hair or protrusions. He did say that it could have but it was wet and anything like that could have looked smooth. Definitely not scaly like a fish, more like the smooth skin of a dolphin or whale.

The creature didn't make any sounds and they didn't notice any panting or breathing. They did not see the body or anything else come out of the water but it was creating a slight wake and a rise in the water in front of it as it moved along. I asked why he didn't move to the edge of the boat to see what it looked like under the water. He didn't think of it at the time and besides didn't want to get that close to it. I remember him saying that it startled them and they were both surprised and a bit scared.

After a few minutes he said it peeled away and slipped back into the water and that was it.

I asked him if he made a sketch of the creature at the time. He said that he did to a local newspaper reporter in the coming days and he knows the sketch was passed on to government people. I recalled he said that when they told people the news spread quickly and created quite a furore for a little while. I think he added that they were hounded for more information for some time. That's all he would say about that.

He also added that a number of other fishermen had seen it or something similar around that time as well, not just them. Conversation moved to his cousins over at Flinders who were out fishing and saw a serpent like creature a few weeks later. This was most likely the sighting by B Hoppen and J Mannix at Flinders whom he was referring to at the time.

I slipped out of the room and came back with a book. I showed him a classic picture of a plesiosaurus. He looked at it and pointed to the head area and said that it was similar but not quite the same. The head was bigger and rounder. Then added again he didn't know about the rest of it as it was under the water.

He never mentioned that H Hoppen apparently shot at it twice with a rifle (as reported in the newspapers), why I don't know, probably because he didn't want to suffer the stigma from the younger generation who generally wouldn't have done that, it was a different time back then I guess.

I'm told H Hoppen was asked about the sighting later in life and he said basically the same thing. He mentioned that they were quite scared and it took them a while to process the information and get past it all.

So that's the full story. Obviously, the details of a second hand account 83 years after the event must be subject to reservations. Nevertheless, considering the wording of the original report, we are probably safe in saying that it was not a known animal.

[62] You will note the reference to a sketch. Frustratingly, no newspaper bothered to publish it, although it was reported[117] that Mr Hoppen's sketch was identical to that drawn independently by Henry Sononi, and both depicted "huge-headed monsters". Who was Henry Sononi? He was a witness who, inspired by the publicity, came forth to describe what he had related to his family a few years before. Off the Lonsdale Reef ie to site of the Hoppens' adventure, he had seen a serpent 12 feet [3.6 metres] long, which was very timid, and refused to take the shark hook he baited for it. He claimed it had "eyes like saucers and a round, foolish face". He scoffed at the idea that it could have been a leopard seal. All of the numerous seals he had seen possessed dog-like heads, whereas this creature's head was big and round, "like a great cannon ball or diver's helmet". That's interesting, because you will remember that the animal seen in Portland Bay in June had a head like a giraffe's.

[63] But back to the year at hand. Towards the end of July a Mr. J. Davis saw another strange creature lying on the fringe of the surf at Airey's Inlet.

[T]he body was about 10 or 12 ft. [3 or 3½ m] long, and about 2½ or 3½ ft. [75 to 105 cm] in girth. The head was a light grey in colour, and it had a sparse coat of darker coloured hair. It had big eyes like those of the Queenscliff monster, but there were no stripes on the body. The head was round.[118]

There can be no doubt this time: it was a leopard seal. Nevertheless, Airey's Inlet was to be visited by a real sea serpent 38 years later, as we shall see.

[64] What about J. Mannix and B. Hoppen, mentioned by the grandson? On 3 August they claimed to have seen a monster 40 feet [12 metres] long, with a snakelike fin 11 feet [3.3 metres] long 4 miles [6½ km] off West Head, near Flinders.[119] Here is B. Hoppen's account:

> "We have both become so accustomed to sea serpent stories that neither of us was startled much when the pale head of what seemed to be a great black snake came out of the water. We saw it first 500 yards away, then it reappeared 400 yards closer, and then again only 25 yards distant. At that range we could see that the black column which drooped realistically like a snake's head, was the tip of some form of growth or a fin on the back."

The following day they saw it again in the company of a "blackfish" or killer whale. 11 feet seems a rather precise measurement for something seen at a distance. Most people would guess 10 feet. If it drooped like a snake's head, it must have stood vertically. If such, it is hard to see how such a projection could have been missed on the earlier sightings. Also, the head was pale, not black. Incredibly as it may sound, it appears to have been different from the other animals sighted. "Curiouser and curiouser," said Alice.

[65] For the final encounter of the year, we must head north. Every Sydneysider knows Cronulla, now their southernmost suburb, but then a separate seaside town. Mr Bransgrove was one of five adults and perhaps seven children disporting themselves in the Oak Park ocean pool near Cronulla shortly before 4 o'clock in the afternoon of Monday 9th December, and was lucky enough to be gazing out to sea when suddenly, to his utter amazement, a long tapering neck, topped by a snake-like head shot out of the water nearby like a pole. It was at least 8 feet [2½ metres] high, and appeared to be mottled in colour. Close in front of it swam a school of porpoises, which it was apparently chasing.

He let out a shout, which alerted four of the others. One of them, a Mr Cheetham said that, following the shout, he saw the head and neck arise about 100 yards out to sea, after which it disappeared and reappeared several times, each time further out, until it was lost to sight. Admitting that he did not have a clear view, he offered the tentative explanation that it might have been a feral deer swimming out from the adjacent Royal National Park. Nonsense! said Bransgrove, who had had a good, clear view. It was too big for a deer, and swam much too fast (not to mention, I might add, that a deer is hardly likely to head for the open ocean).[120]

And so ended two remarkable years. Sea serpents stayed away from Australian coasts for the remainder of the 1930s, although they put in several appearances off New Zealand in the middle of 1939.[121] But then the world went to war, and people had more important things to talk about than sea serpents. When the tumult and the fighting were done, the world had changed, and people had forgotten that it had once been respectable to see and report on sea serpents, and at least have one's words taken seriously.

But they never really went away.

9. Sea Serpents of the Top End

From now on it is more convenient to tell the story topographically rather than chronologically. The far north of Australia is sparsely occupied, and I suspect that if there were more large coastal towns, sightings would be much more common. (See Map 1 on page 101 for the relevant locations.)

[66] In 1934, in the wake of publicity about the Loch Ness Monster, Captain T. W. Arthur decided to tell what happened to him on Saturday 3 June 1916[122]. A point in his favour was that he spent a lot of time describing the small details of the voyage, while providing only a few on the monster itself. A hoaxer would be more likely to do the reverse.

Captain Arthur claimed to have spent half a century on or near the sea, from the Arctic to the Antarctic, and many places in between. During the First World War he was involved in the construction of lighthouses at Darwin and Cape Don, on the Coburg Peninsula. An internet search confirms that the latter was built during the period 1915 to 1917. On the King's Birthday long weekend he and seven others decided to take a visit to Melville Island, 18 miles [29 km] away across the Dundas Strait, so they loaded up some provisions, rifles, and ammunition onto a 27 foot [8¼ metres] long surf boat and set off about 3 pm. He goes into detail about the speed and the tide, and tells how, about 6.30 pm a trawler captain called Ned Baxter was on the bow keeping a lookout for Elphinstone Reef, said by the chart to be at 11° 10'S, 131.25° E.

> I was steering with the big sweep oar, when Baxter shouted out to me "What's that just astern there?" I turned sharply, thinking it was rocks when to my surprise, and not more than 30 feet [9 m] from me, appeared a huge head about 6 feet [1.8 m] out of the water, and with 5 or 6 large parts of its body in a straight line with a division between each of them, reaching in all about 40 feet [12 m]. As it came nearer I lifted the blade of my oar as high out of the water as I could and tried to hit it on the head, which by

this time was only a foot about the water. I missed hitting it, but felt a hard jerk on my oar blade which nearly knocked me over the side.

The animal had disappeared, but they discovered four teeth embedded in the oar, three on one side and one on the other. They kept them as souvenirs, two of which he claimed to still have in his possession. Considering what remarkable items these would have been, it is a pity no journalist asked to see them. Be that as it may, he then went on to relate their subsequent adventures, which provide no additional details to the sighting, but simply add to the impression that he is describing a real event. He said they fell asleep exhausted on the beach at Cape Fleeming, then returned to their embarkation point "after three days' terrible experience without water and adrift in a heavy sea", and how the biggest and strongest of the group, a man called Milliken collapsed and died soon after their return.

[67] For the next story, you must understand that Bernard Heuvelmans' book, *In the Wake of the Sea-Serpents* was first published in English in 1968. On 23 November 1980 the *Sun-Herald* (Sydney) published a review of the book after it had been republished, an act which inspired a letter to the editor the following Sunday from ex-Leading Seaman Cecil W. Walters about an experience of his in 1939 on board H.M.A.S. *Kurumba*.[123] The letter was discovered by my friend, Paul Cropper, who was able to interview Mr Walters on 15 January 1989.[124] It turned out that Mr Walters had already made notes of the incident in 1969 after reading a review of the first edition of Heuvelmans' book, and since they are twenty years closer to the event, and contain all the details in the 1980 letter, they are transcribed as follows:

> About the middle of October 1939, while serving as a gunner on a naval oil tanker proceeding from Darwin, I had what I now realise to be a most remarkable experience in as such as I saw a real sea serpent. As we were app. 2 days out of Darwin there was no question of my sobriety which is always brought up when I speak of this occurrence. What is more I did have one person to

corroborate my story, unfortunately he was killed in the war. Perhaps others saw it or were told them of it no doubt, but I do not remember names as I left the ship at Fremantle and have seen no more of them since.

We were somewhere N.W. of King Sound around East Longitude 114 Lat 20 South W heading South West 10 knots. It was about 2 bells in the afternoon watch when we sighted the object on the starboard quarter about 4 miles distant overtaking us quite fast on a roughly parallel course. Not being experienced in such matters I can only guess its speed at about 20 knots. I trained the gun on it and looking through the telescope I saw the serpent plainer. It appeared in three half loops thus, 10 feet out of the water 30 feet from loop to loop. The body thick as a man's and marked exactly like a giraffe, pale blue, green, yellow patched and small ears flat on the head. We watched for about half an hour until it disappeared in the haze on our starboard bow. I decided to write this because of the mention of anthropologist looking for the sea serpent.   (Signed) C. Walters.

As an officer of the Department of Veterans' Affairs, I was able to confirm from the record of ships' movements, that the *Kurumba* was a tanker, and it left Darwin on 7 October 1939 to arrive at Fremantle on 16th of the month, so it probably would have taken four or five days, not two, to reach the site. I have listened to the tape of the interview in which further information was obtained. The demeanour of the witness, as well as the fact that the notes had been written for personal reference, all mitigate against a hoax.

2 bells is 1 p.m. The weather was fine but hazy. He and a seaman called Jack Mack were on anti-submarine watch at the stern gun, which was flanked on either side by a telescope. The importance of this is that the telescopes were calibrated for distance, making his estimate of distance accurate, and they were strong enough to provide a good view of the object. It was moving so fast that initially he mistook it for a mechanical object. The presence of a bow wave indicated a speed of at least 10 knots [18½ k.p.h.], and since it was overtaking the ship, itself travelling at 10 knots, a minimum estimate of its speed would have been 15 knots. Its course was slightly divergent from that of the ship.

Fig 8A. Mr Walters' 1969 sketch of the *Kurumba* sea serpent

Fig. 8B. Preliminary sketches of the head, 1989

Fig. 8C. Final sketch of the head and neck

He confirmed the size mentioned in his notes, and because of the distance it is unlikely to have been underestimated. Thus, the *visible* parts alone would have been 90 feet, or 27½ metres - as long as the largest whale. He could discern neither tail, fins, nor limbs, nor any means of propulsion, and the loops maintained the same relative position throughout, without moving.

What was really striking was the colouration. Against a background of brownish yellow, like a withered leaf, was superimposed a multi-coloured giraffe-like pattern, Also, dark greenish patches existed over the eye, around the nostril, as on the ear. The pattern was like matt paint, but very distinct in the contrasting colours, and the surface was definitely skin, not metallic.

The head did not move, nor was there any obvious division between it and the neck. Although the mouth was not open, the jaws were constantly "working" and the tongue constantly flicking in and out, and the witness particularly noticed a dainty little ear tucked back behind the eye.

No doubt the interval of 30 years for the notes and 50 years for the interview will have affected his memory, and we may question some of the details, but it does not alter the fact that this was a quite extraordinary sighting. And to think we have this record only because he wrote a single paragraph to a newspaper, and an eagle-eyed researcher found it!

[68] I find the next story really frustrating, because I have not been able to locate the original article. *Trove*'s data on digitalised newspapers run out a year or two beforehand.   Nevertheless, the date was apparently Tuesday 10 May 1955, based on a brief mention in *The Canberra Times* :

DARWIN, Wednesday.   Two Darwin women claimed they saw a sea monster in Darwin Harbour yesterday. They described the monster as a series of black dots stretching over 100 yards with a hump rising and falling beneath the waves. Three children notified the police of the same thing.[125]

[69] No doubt it is the lack of large towns in the far north which is responsible for the Darwin area dominating the sea serpent reports. 1959 was the year of the "Mandorah Monster," Mandorah being a tiny village just across the harbour, only 6 or 7 km from the nearest point of Darwin. A few kilometres down the coast a very narrow estuary called Woods Inlet leads inland to the Aboriginal community of Beluen, which at the time was known an Delissaville.

The news broke on 13 October[126], when Commander H. O. B. Hodgson confirmed that the navy had been searching the harbour for an object reported to them three times. The first was when Mr Alan Carter (or Allan; the press spelled his name both ways), who ran the Mandorah holiday resort, called in by radio and reported that, in the evening, he had seen "a long black shallow object travelling just above or close to the surface" between Mandorah and Doctor's Gully, the part of Darwin opposite Mandorah, at an estimated speed of 90 miles per hour [145 kph] which is, to put in mildly, a bit on the high side for a living creature. Amazingly, a green light shone into the sky as it was heading towards Delissaville. The next morning he saw it again, moving towards one of the creeks on his (western) side of the harbour. Ten days after his report, a Mr. J. G. Slaggert saw a "strange looking monster" near Mandorah, and stated "It was either some kind of low flying object or monster." He could not hear anything which sounded like a motor "only a queer swooshing noise like giant wings or a new type of jet."

Needless to say, the newspaper omitted such trivial details as distance, length of sightings, lighting and visibility, but did state that the length was estimated at 80 to 100 feet [24 - 30 m]. Enter Ted Maloney, who'd been fishing the waters of Tasmania, the Barrier Reef and the Northern Territory for 18 years. He'd seen the monster plenty of times, he said. It was a giant ray, the biggest he'd ever seen, but friendly and harmless. It was 25 feet [7.6 m] across, and at least 40 feet [12.3 m] long, including its tail. However, it was easy to overestimate its size, he added (not without reason, for he himself had obviously just done so). Seen in clear water, at a distance, with its shadow behind it could easily appear the reported length of the Mandorah monster. (Of course, there wouldn't have been any shadow at night, when Mr Carter saw it.) Its top speed was 40 mph [65 kph - another exaggeration] but appeared faster.[127]

The following week a Mrs Dorothy de Fraine told how, when she was managing the Seabreeze Hotel in 1955, she saw a gigantic manta ray stranded in the shallows at Seabreeze Point, rolling itself into a ball and floundering, trying to get into deeper water, which it eventually succeeding in doing. It was a dirty black and grey in colour, with white underparts, and its two fins were 12 to 14 feet [3.6 to 4.2 metres] apart.[128] A couple of days later she came up with the interesting snippet of information that, in 1954 ie a year before the manta stranding, a strange green light similar to what Mr Carter had seen rose up over the ocean near the Seabreeze Hotel.[129] The following Sunday, a fisherman called Ian Harper encountered a huge, jet black ray basking in the sun off Shoal Bay on the north shore of Darwin. He circled it in his 18 foot [5½ metre] launch, and estimated its span at 20 to 25 feet [6 to 7½ metres], which I suspect was an exaggeration.

Finally, Mr Carter came forward and declared that what he had seen was no animal. Himself a former wartime test pilot, he claimed that his object had possessed a superstructure, and was definitely mechanically driven. It had been 90 to 100 feet long and, although it produced no noise, it had raced along at 80 to 90 miles an hour without leaving a wake. He also said that on that first day a woman had observed it through binoculars, and her description tallied with his.[130]

Personally, I think that all the discussion about huge rays is a red herring distracting us from what Carter and Slaggert actually saw. By the time I was able to catch up with Mr Carter, he was too old to be of any help. Nevertheless, we must take into consideration his, and Slaggert's description of the object at the time and, of course, the green light - which also appeared four years before. In my opinion, this was not a sea monster at all, but something even stranger: a UFO!

[70] Just the same, a real sea monster may have visited the area in the period 1974 to 1982, because in 2001 reporter Peter Cain wrote an article about sightings dating from just before Cyclone Tracy, but which hadn't occurred "for at least 18 years". Five anonymous witnesses had been interviewed separately over a period of six months. All the sightings had taken place between the *Song Saigon* artificial reef and the mouth of Woods Inlet. The latter, you will remember, is a short distance south of Mandorah, while the artificial reef is based around a Vietnamese refugee ship deliberately sunk there in 1982, about 5 km south east of Mandorah.

> All [sightings] were in the later afternoon or early evening but in reasonable light conditions - and importantly, none of the witnesses were all that far away from whatever it was. Three were within 60 - 100 m, one about 150m and the other about 400m. All say it was the same colour, a drab, olive green although the closer witnesses say the creature's "shell" may have had a mottled pattern. All said the body appeared to be made up of a series of interconnecting plates much like a Moreton Bay bug or a series of overlapping turtle shells. From here, the accounts begin to differ slightly. On length, for a start - estimates of length ranged from 10m to about 20m, with the furthest sighting going even higher. Not all saw the head but those who did claimed the monster had nostrils on top of a snout and large eyes. One witness claimed the thing had short, floppy ears - but that description came after the Esky had been emptied, so that description may be unreliable. One witness described the swimming motion as being like a huge tractor tyre rolling along the top of the water, tread up. Two of the witnesses said it was moving very rapidly, like it was feeding on a school of fast-moving fish.[131]

[71] The scene now shifts to a small Aboriginal community in the middle of the northern coast of Arnhem Land, at the mouth of the Liverpool River. In 1972 the southern newspapers carried a brief paragraph about how the Maningrida monster had returned, and cited the *Maningrida Mirage*. So, when I finally got to Darwin, I went to the library to seek out this august publication. It turned out to be a mimeographed newsletter. Here, then, is the full account.[132]

An extraordinary report has reached the Mirage of two local Maningrida residents having again sighted the fabled Maningrida monster near the mouth of the Gudjerama Creek. This strange sea creature, which to date defies description, has not been seen for a number of years. Positive identification has never yet been made due to the elusive and nocturnal nature of the amphibian. A number of noted marine biologists and other scientists have attempted to sort out the mystery, but as none of them has actually ever seen the creature they are all understandably sceptical about the whole situation and no official comment has been made.

On this present occasion, the two men were fishing when a tremendous disturbance occurred in the area about three-quarters of a mile distant. It was first noticed as a wide area of boiling frothing water followed by sections of the animal appearing above the disturbance. Egrets, terns and other water birds for a radius of hundreds of yards were frightened into the air. As in most earlier sightings, the disturbance was accompanied with a characteristic sustained high pitched moaning, a cross between the howl of a dingo and a bellowing elephant.

It was not possible to ascertain the creature's exact colour except that it was generally dark, and there appeared to be glistening sections as the sun was being reflected from incredibly large metallic-looking scales. As fantastic as it seemed then and does now in retrospect, it was felt by the two fishermen, that the creature's head, if it could be called that, was in fact in three sections, almost similar to the sections on a three-bladed propeller with all parts being centrally attached to the body.

It was thought that the length of the serpentine animal could have been in excess of one hundred feet. However, the men felt that due to the amount of disturbance caused by the creature's thrashing about that the length may have been a more conservative fifty to sixty feet. It was not possible to guess the thickness of the body. This eminently intriguing mystery was evident on this occasion for about 15 to 20 minutes before it finally subsided.

It then continues with references to earlier witnesses, without providing any details. You will, of course, immediately note the suspicious combination of a completely fantastic story and complete anonymity of the witnesses - despite being in a community small enough for everyone to know everybody else's business. I made a few enquiries, and finally a national parks officer, Dan Guillespie informed me that it had been a practical joke by a schoolteacher. I'm not prepared to dispute it.

[72] "Dinosaur Found in NT Harbor" was the front page headline in *The Northern Territory News* of 2 February 1980.[133] It was not Darwin Harbour they were talking about, but Bynoe Harbour, a narrow inlet to the west of, and parallel to, Darwin Harbour, separated from it by the Cox Peninsula. A local businessman, Burge Brown declared that the harbour was a centre for "plesiosaurs", but he had seen them only during the wet season, December to February. The last time was about two years before (? late 1977 or early 1978), when he was with a small party fishing in deep water off Rankin Point, which is situated about halfway down the inlet.

The day was still when, without any apparent reason, fish and sea snakes began leaping out of the water. Just then the monster came heading towards them "like a submarine". He described it as having a tail and front like an elephant's trunk, with a pair of dorsal fins running down its back, which fascinated him because they were not rigid, but "flopped about".

One of his companions, Police Sergeant Kevin Maley confirmed that it was the most incredible thing he had ever seen. It was black, and about 30 m long, with a head the size of a football. Surprising, it kept within 20 metres of them for about 20 minutes, and just stared at the boat without being at all aggressive. Another companion, Jack Davis was in another boat in another part of the harbour, and so missed the visitation, although he did confirm that as they were coming back to where Burge was, the water was "a funny color as though it was all stirred up", with yellow sea snakes on the surface. Then Burge called out that they had seen the monster.

Burge Brown also said that, about a year before that he and his son, Geoffrey were searching for the wreckage of a boat when they heard a bellow like a bull being branded, causing the dogs to panic and flee. A quarter of an hour later he looked over and saw three of those monsters about 800 metres away, so he used his field glasses on them. He considered the big one to be 30 meters long, and they were "moving along in water up to their guts."

By the time I began researching it in early 1989, Burge Brown had already passed away, but Kevin Maley was prepared to discuss it. He confirmed that the animal surfaced less than 20 metres from them, and just lay there for 20 minutes before submerging. The newspaper article was basically accurate, except that he insisted the size was grossly exaggerated. It was more like 24 or 25 feet [7½ m]. (Note that metrication was a relative novelty at the time, and most of us were used to thinking in imperial measures. Although the paper said "30 m", what Maley had probably told them was "30 feet")

The body displayed no obvious humps, but it did possess three (not two) rows of triangular fins not unlike those of a crocodile except that they were floppy. Had they been erect, they might have been 6 inches [15 cm] high. The thin neck was about 8 or 10 feet [2½ to 3 m] long, but possessed a vertical S-bend like a sewage pipe, held close to the surface rather than towering upright. He did not notice any features on the head, which was the size of a turtle's.

[73] That story encouraged a Mr R. M. E. Richardson to tell his.[134] It was during the term of office of Mick Driver as NT Administrator, 1946 to 1950 ie 30 years beforehand. He had been walking on a cliff near Larrekeyah Barracks ie on the southern shore of Darwin, when he saw what appeared to be three logs, about 8 metres long and black, floating off Larrekeyah Point. Much to his surprise, he realised that they were alive and swimming. One of them raised its head like a tiger snake ready to strike. The interesting thing was that , when he mentioned this to Mr Driver on a visit to Government House a few days later, the

Administrator gave a name to them, and told him he was very lucky to see them, as they rarely visited Top End waters.

[74] That wasn't all. About 11 am on Wednesday 20 February 1980 ie less than a week after the last report, the newspaper received a phone call from two insurance officers, Terry Annesley and John Hamilton to announce that a mystery sea creature could be seen from the Hooker Building.[135] Journalist Fred McCue and photographer, Keith Scott hurried over, to see several humps protruding from the water about a kilometre away. The object was moving at a fairly consistent rate out of the harbour, and the two insurance officers told it had moved about 1½ km since they had first seen it.

When another journalist, David Trounce arrived with a set of binoculars, they were able to repair to the top of the building and take turns gazing at the object closely. McCue got the impression that it was a dark object about 15 m long with a series of dorsal fins, but it was far too big for a dolphin and the wrong shape for a manta ray. Trounce counted five fins at one stage, but they were far too close together to belong to a series of dolphins. Instead, it appeared to be a single eel-like object.

So what was it? In fairness, it should be mentioned that Mr McCue later told me that he had reservations about it, and only wrote the story on orders from his editor. But there still seems to be no obvious identification.

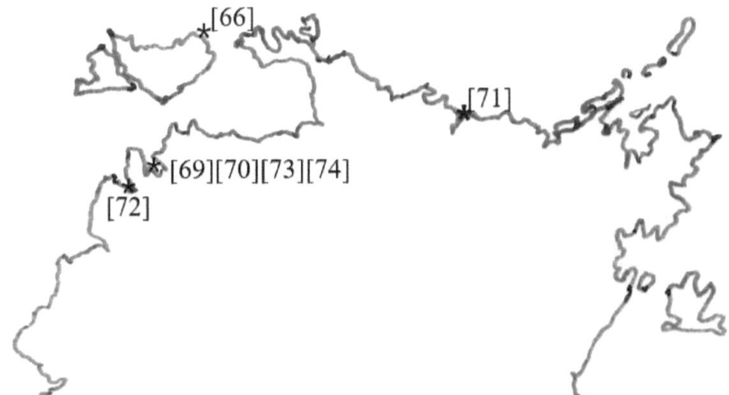

Map 1. Northern Territory Coast (Top End)

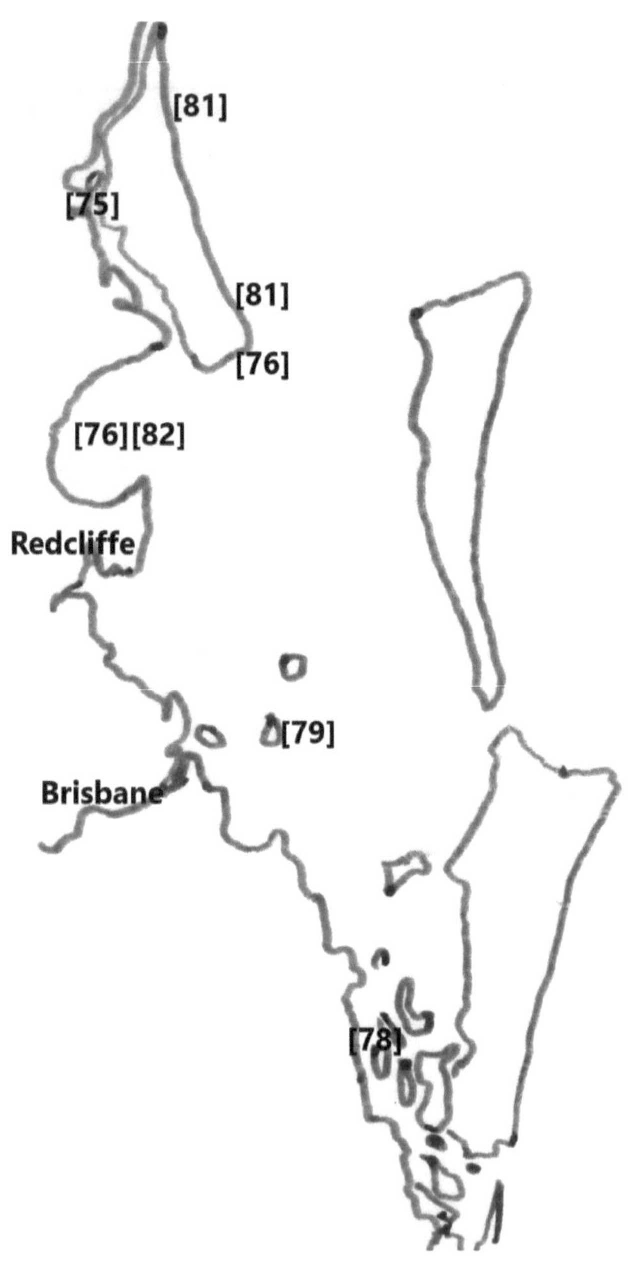

Map 2. Moreton Bay, Queensland

10. Deception Bay and Bribie Island

Deception Bay is close to where I live, and I can never see the name without thinking, "Monster". This is because my family moved to a northern suburb of Brisbane when I was a little boy, and the first time I heard the name was when the now defunct Sunday paper, the *Truth* published a series of articles about an inquisitive monster there. Then, twenty-nine years later, I reread Heuvelmans' book and saw a reference to Nigel Tutt of Hendra as a witness. Did he still live there? I wondered. He did! Not only that, but he was only too happy to tell me the story in writing and face to face, and to get me in touch with his daughter and fellow witness, Carol Borck, and to allow me to copy all the original newspaper articles about it.[136]

To set the stage, Moreton Bay, on which Brisbane is situated, consists of a number of sub-bays, as shown in Map 2 on the previous page. The northern boundary of Brisbane City is formed by the mouth of the Pine River, beyond which juts the Redcliffe Peninsula. Deception Bay forms an almost semicircular arc to the north of that, bounded on the south by Redcliffe, and to the north by Bribie Island, with the Caboolture River entering the bay about halfway between them. Bribie Island itself is a narrow, north-south island, inhabited only on the southern tip, and separated from the mainland by the very narrow Pumicestone Passage. Toorbul is a village on the mainland close to the southern opening of the passage.

[75] But before we get to the main event, let us look at what happened in November 1948 which, although not an honest -to-goodness sea serpent event, is still rather perplexing. At the White Patch reef, 10 km north of Toorbul, in the Passage, a boat hirer called Mr. A. J. Felschow had a snake approach within three to six feet [90 to 180 cm] and make a squeaky sound like a mouse.[137] Despite people's tendency to exaggerate, one would expect that a good estimate of its length could be made at such a short range. It was 18 to 24 feet [5.5 to 7.3 metres] long. They

hauled up the anchor and get out of there, but not before he noted that it was brown in colour, with eyes as big as pennies (we'd say 20c pieces these days), three inches [7½ cm] thick, and with a head "seven inches long, five inches wide, and three inches thick". That's 17½ x 12½ x 7½ centimetres, or about the size of two hands placed together.

The animal was obviously a snake, but I am at a loss to decide which one. No sea snake is anywhere near that length. Quite a few pythons could be classed as brown, but they seldom reach that length and, although they occasionally end up in water, it is not their normal habitat.

To complicate matters, Mr W. Burns also claimed to have seen "the serpent" on November 17 and 19, only it was yellow like a ripe banana, made a loud hiss, and was accompanied by five young ones. The length was not mentioned, but it sounds like the yellow-bellied sea snake, *Pelamis platura*, the most widely distributed of all sea snakes. It is surprising that its dark back was not mentioned, but some individuals are yellow all over except for a narrow dark strip down the back.

On 13 December, a Member of Parliament, Mr. E. P. Decker, with the help of a Gilbert Jones, caught a genuine sea snake just off White Patch beach.[138] This one was brown, but only five feet [1½ metres] long. To make matters more interesting, two days after the original story, a Mr. C. Bungey came forth and claimed that the "Toorbul Point monster" was an outsized turtle. He had seen it in early November, and about a dozen times since 1944, and said:

> "It's the size of a fair-sized table, and rears out of the water abut 2ft. 6in. [76 cm]. It has a yellow back with black stripes and a tremendous head."[139]

With due allowances to be made for its appearance of colour in the water, this sounds like a leatherback turtle, *Dermochelys coriacae*, the largest of the world's sea turtles.

[76] Now let's go forward eleven years to something a lot more interesting. The first was an article[140] on 3 January 1960 reporting the experiences of three young people: Ron Spencer, 22, his wife, Jeanette, 21 and his friend, John Belcher, 22. Ron said he had been fishing in Deception Bay for eight years, and had seen sea cows, porpoises, and turtles, but five times in the previous twelve months something else was in the water. It would come up close to the boat, as if curious about it, then dive, but reappear several times, following the boat. Its head was about 18 inches to two feet [45 to 60 cm] wide, a brownish colour, without any obvious neck, and strange, staring eyes. His wife told the paper that she had been out fishing with him nine months before when a "huge, black thing" came out of the water, and she got to her husband to take her back to shore. And according to John Belcher:

"I saw it about two weeks ago when I was out fishing with Ron. At first, I thought it might be a turtle, but when I had a proper look I saw that it was not. Its head is far too big for a turtle's. It is a tannish brown color and it just comes out of the water, looks about and goes away again."

It is only fair to add, however, that when I telephoned Mr Belcher in 1996, he said he was indignant at the newspaper report, and what he had seen was a sea cow, or dugong, of which there are quite a few in Moreton Bay.

Around the same time, another newspaper ran a short paragraph[141] about a Mr. N. Tutt, who had a mottled brown eel-like creature 18 feet [5½ metres] long and 3 feet [90 cm] wide, with a square head, approach his dinghy at 12.15 the day before, while he was fishing with his daughter and her friend. The site was not mentioned. A week after the initial article, the *Truth* reported that its lines had been running hot with stories[142]. One was from Nigel Tutt, who owned a holiday home at Deception Bay, and who was now frequenting the bay with a camera, hoping to see again the "monster" which surfaced four times out of the water, the last one just eight feet [2½ metres] from his boat. It was 18 to 20 feet long, with a square head, brown, and with a yellow mouth. More about Mr Tutt later.

Later, a Dave Manners reported seeing a monster with "the ugliest head he has ever seen." For your reference, Skirmish Point is at the southeast tip of Bribie Island.

> "The head is round, something like a man's, at least 2 ft. 6 in. [76 cm] across and 2 ft. [61 cm] long, with a flat nose and sort of semi-detached to the body," he said today. "The body is about 25 ft. [7.6 m] long."
>
> Dave, 26, a Railway Department night officer holidaying at Bribie Island, and his mother, Mrs. I. Manners, saw the "monster" at 7.20 a.m. today.
>
> "We were quietly beach fishing in Woody Bay near Skirmish Point, two miles south of of Ocean Beach, when we first saw it," Dave said. "It surfaced about 20 yards off-shore and was clearly visible in the shallow water," he said. "I dropped my rod, and Mum and I followed it at walking pace for about 1½ miles [2.4 km] before we went to breakfast. It was a dirty brown color and appeared to have a body about 2 ft. across and a queer-looking fin 18 ft. from the head. It kept surfacing about every 50 yards."
>
> Dave said that several other fishermen saw the "monster" and could not identify it.

If the body was 25 feet long, he would hardly have described the fin as 18 feet from the head; 18 *inches* [46 cm] was almost certainly intended. Also, on the basis of the following report, I suspect he included the neck with the head.

Some time in September, the *Truth*, for a bit of fun, ran a contest for accounts of monster seen in Queensland or its waters. The results surprised even them: they ended up with three weeks' of the wildest, tallest tales you could imagine. Anyone who wants to know how to recognize a genuine, if perhaps mistaken, story of a mystery animal from a hoax could do worse than read those tales. In the end, the winner was our earlier informant, Nigel Tutt[143]. For this, his prize was 21 guineas, which equates to $655 in 2018[144]. *And* he got a baby crocodile, which he called Huey, and fed it on butcher's mince until it died. However, he did spend the prize money on a new camera, and built a special waterproof chamber for it in his boat, but the monster never turned up again.

The three witnesses were Nigel, his 15-year-old daughter, Carol, and her friend, Joy Zeller. And here we have a good example of the heritability of memory. Joy was unable to provide any details except to confirm the event, and the fact that the creature was big and frightening. However, Nigel was able to add extra details twenty-nine years after the event, while Carol also gave a good account of it, even though she now lived in a different state, and did not have the original newspaper clippings to refresh her memory. "That creature has always been very vivid in my memory," she said at a later date. Likewise, both Nigel and his brother were able to provide detailed accounts of a huge cat they saw before the war. The following is a combination of Nigel's detailed newspaper stories, along with his, and Carol's accounts in 1989.

It took place on New Year's Day - both agreed on that. The sky was very clear, the sea calm, and the tide full. In his 1960 account, Nigel related how they had gone out to look at the black swans near the mouth of the Caboolture River, then headed to the edge of the shipping channel, throttled the engine back, and handed the tiller to the girls.

"Then suddenly, right in front of our bows, a huge, square-shaped head rose up about four feet [1.2 m] out of the water. The girls let out a shriek and turned the tiller so hard they nearly tied the boat in three knots. 'Plop' - the head disappeared. When we straightened things out again I felt disappointed at not getting a clearer view of the thing. So I decided to run the launch a couple of circles in case it should surface again. Sure enough, it was most obliging. It came up three more times. In fact, it seemed quite a friendly creature - I'm sure it liked people. Its body was of two shades of brown, in big mottles, and its skin looked lumpy, not scaly. Its head was square-shaped, and hard to describe. But if you've ever seen the boot of a Mayflower car - well, it was something the shape of that. It had a yellow mouth, and appeared to have nostrils.

"As it was acting so friendly, we decided to make for shore and get a camera. So I opened the outboard motor out, and after 10 minutes decided the Monster must have been left behind. But then came the best view we had of him - there he was, curving and gliding calmly along beside the boat and only about 8 ft. [2.4 m] away, about 22 ft. long and as thick as a sack of corn, with a fin about 6 ft. to 8 ft. [1.8 - 2.4 m] back from its head. I thought, 'could he be a giant eel, the daddy of them all?' but an eel swims with a sideways motion, and this fellow was undulating up and down."

That last statement is important. He particularly emphasized it in his 1989 statements, and on being questioned, felt that the undulations - five or six at the most - were each as long as a man's arm, and about 30 cm out of the water, but there were definitely no humps. Carol also remembered its movements as like a person swimming breaststroke, its body moving up and down at the same time. The significance of this is that only mammals swim in this way.

Fig. 9. Nigel Tutt's 1986 sketch of what he saw on New Year's Day, 1960

To continue with their later statements: Carol also recalled the monster appearing just as her father had given her a turn at steering. She didn't get the impression that it was at all aggressive, but she was terrified it might capsize the boat. Nigel informed me that, at the time of the monster's first appearance, it was about "a cricket pitch", or 20 metres, away. It had suddenly thrust its head almost vertically about 4 feet [120 cm] out of the water. It then went under water, and he was disappointed not to have a better view, but as he eased the boat in a wide circle, it surfaced three more times, but not as high as before, swimming about 6 metres away, parallel to the boat, until it finally surfaced just 8 feet, or 2.4 metres away.

His boat was 13 feet [4 metres] long, and since its head protruded beyond the bow and its tail beyond the stern, he estimated its length at 18 to 20 feet [5½ to 6 metres]. Carol also said it was longer than the boat. Both agreed that it was thickset - elongated, but not really serpentine in appearance. Nigel did not get a good look at the tail, but he did not think it was lobed.

The skin appeared "slimy" or "wet", but definitely not furred, and gave the appearance of being extremely coarse, or rather, lumpy looking. ("Like that of a cane toad, but magnified," said Carol.) The colour was a very dark, mottled brown, with the underside of the chin a lighter brown, but they did not see the belly. The head was about 2 feet [60 cm] wide, and almost square, with a square muzzle. When it opened its mouth, Carol started thinking of Jonah and the whale. Nigel said it was wide, with the configuration of a fresh water catfish. He did not remember teeth or tongue, but did recall, as mentioned in 1960, that it was yellow!

They did not recall any vibrissae, or whiskers, but both did remember eyes and nostrils. Nigel thought the nostrils were widely spaced just a little bit above the mouth.

Nigel remembered a neck slightly longer than the head, and just a little narrower - but still definitely a neck, rather than a mere continuation of the body as with an eel. The "fins" were positioned on the body ie behind the neck, at the sides, but higher than the centre line. He thought they were a foot [30 cm] long and wide, and somewhat rounded. They were also fleshy, clearly possessing a bony structure, as distinct from the rays and skin of a fish.

At the end of the interview, I showed him the chart of "Pinnipeds around the world" from the April 1987 issue of the *National Geographic*. Pinnipeds are seals and sea lions. He pointed to the leopard seal (*Hydrurga leptonynx*) as not unlike it in profile. The neck of the monster was comparatively thicker than the leopard seal's, but about the right length. The monster was comparatively more elongated. The colouration was similar, but the placing of the fins wrong. The shape of the leopard seal's fins (actually, its flippers) are somewhat the right shape, but the "monster's" fins were rounder and shorter.

Just the same, we might still ask whether it was, in fact, a leopard seal. If so, it was exceptionally large. The length of the four metre boat would represent the normal maximum for a leopard seal - and you will remember Dave Manners' estimate was even higher. A leopard seal's skin is furred, and could never be compared to a cane toad's, while its colour is dark grey with darker blotches, not brown. Its head is pointed, flattened, even triangular, but never square. It would be unusual for its teeth not to be visible when it opened its mouth and, of course, like any other self-respecting mammal, its mouth is pink, not yellow.

No, it is pretty clear that whatever made Deception Bay its home in 1959 and 1960, it was not a known species. We will discuss its identity further in the last chapter.

[77] But that's not all. I told you that the "monster" contest produced some really tall tales, but there were also a few short paragraphs which had the ring of truth. Like this one:-

> Another story this week comes to us from New South Wales - from Mrs. M. L. Carr, a former Queenslander, now living at Williamtown Air Force Base. She told us about a Monster she once saw in the water on a reef near Bribie Island, "with a big body and neck, poised as if staring up at me."[145]

And this [78]:

> Mr. E. J. Bailey, of Beaconsfield-terrace, saw a strange beast in the water off Russell Island in Redland Bay, "like a horse or hippopotamus, with an arched neck, a short back, that moved through the water with great speed and power."[146]

Russell Island is a small island in the southernmost corner of Moreton Bay, and the description sounds like many of the others in this book.

[79] St Helena Island is approximately in the centre of Moreton Bay. The following story sounds a little melodramatic, but I wouldn't reject it out of hand. It comes from page 2 of the issue of 2 October.

Mrs. M. Chadwick, of The Esplanade, Wynnum, saw another "something" in Moreton Bay near St. Helena Island about two years ago [ie 1958] - "It had a large, flat, snake-like head, shiny, and pale green in color, with big wide-apart eyes and a mouth from ear to ear. It kept going (and so did we!)"[147]

[80] Interestingly, in the paragraph right above it in the same edition came a story of an encounter at Sinclair Bay. The bay is about 24 km southeast of Bowen, and may have remembered it from the events of 1934 [55]. In this case, the creature sounds very familiar, and the fact that the author named two other witnesses adds to his credibility.

Mr. Sid Hurst, of Powell-street, Bowen, for example, told us of the day in August 1958, when he and Glen Heron, Harold Brock and Charles Leaver saw a Monster in Sinclair Bay. "In the distance it looked like a huge log," he said. "But as we go closer we could see that it looked like a caterpillar, with a long swan-like neck and a tail like a snake. It was about three times the length of our boat (or about 70 ft [21 metres]) and travelled at a tremendous speed."

[81] The story doesn't end there, because two years later a quite different sea monster turned up off Bribie Island. To be precise, two miles, or three kilometres offshore from Woorim, a village near the southern tip, facing the sea rather the bay, as was reported by Robert ("Bud") Duncan, 68. Duncan, a self-confessed beachcomber at Bribie for fifty years, used powerful binoculars to watch it playing around on the surface, rolling from side to side, for four minutes. This happened a few days before being reported on 26 October.

"It was whitish grey in colour, about 12 feet [3.7 metres] long, and seemed to have a swan's neck, a whale's body, and a fish's tail and fins," Bud said last night. "It repeatedly raised its strange neck out of the water, and then flipped its strange tail. I made a quick sketch of it just to prove to my mates that I wasn't seeing things," he said.[148]

I presume the interview was by telephone, because he apparently did not show the sketch to the newspaper, which had to do with this whimsical, and probably quite inaccurate, artist's impression. It is a pity, however, that the interviewer did not request more details from him.

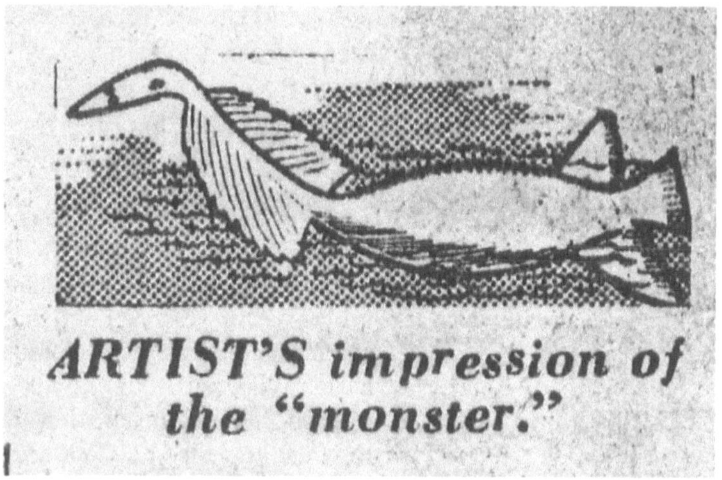

Fig. 10. This newspaper artist's impression may have little resemblance to what Mr. Duncan saw.

Two weeks later, on Monday 8 October, he saw it again, this time ten kilometres from the north end of the island.

He described the monster as having a long, finned neck, shiny body, and fish tail. "He surfaced with a sucking noise and cruised slowly towards the shore," Mr. Duncan said. "Instead of 12 ft. as I first estimated, it was about 20 ft. [6 metres] long. Its snout, instead of being pointed, is flat like a pig's. It has two little holes near the centre. They'd be its nostrils, I suppose."[149]

It must have appeared again in the next couple of months, because in December he was reported to have seen it three times. Also, an amateur fisherman called James Kentworth claimed to have seen "a strange animal" playing in shallow water between Scarborough (the northernmost suburb of Redcliffe) and Deception Bay (presumably the village)[150]. In the absence of further details, one would guess it was the same thing.

[82] The Bay still had its secrets. In December 1996, I was on talkback radio promoting my book, *Bunyips and Bigfoots*. When the compere referred to the section on the Deception Bay monster, a Mr Mick Scheirupflug phoned in to say that he also had encountered a strange animal in the bay. One thing lead to another and, that evening, I was able to interview all three witnesses independently by telephone.

Matters of Agreement. All three agreed on the basic details. Several decades before, Mr Scheirupflug, his son, and a young friend had hired a boat in order to fish for whiting in the bay. The creature surfaced not too far away, and was in view for a few minutes, moving parallel to them. It was a slim, serpentine animal consisting of a series of humps, but with no fins. They had difficulty describing its motion but, after some probing, but not leading, questions they all agreed it moved by vertical undulations. They also all agreed that it finally slid forward into the water and disappeared. They did not mention it to anybody else. Now for the individual stories.

First Witness. Mick Scheirupflug, retired carpenter, aged 77 in 1996. He was vague about the year, but suggested it was about 20 years before. Then his wife chimed in and said it was more like 30 or 40. The event took place about half past 8 in the morning, about half a mile from Scarborough, where the water was only about 3 to 6 metres deep, and calm. The boat was stationary, and the animal about 150 yards away. The sighting lasted 4 or 5 minutes. It was pale brown, mottled like a carpet snake. He thought there were three humps, protruding a couple of feet out of the water, with a total length of well over 20 feet [6 metres]. He could not remember seeing any head or tail.

Second Witness: Peter Scheirupflug, son of Mick, aged 49. As the youngest member of the party, his memory was the weakest, and required a lot of prompting. He told me that afterwards, they convinced themselves they hadn't seen it.

He thinks he was aged 10 or 11 at the time. The time was about 2 pm, and they were drifting about 2 km from Scarborough, the water being very calm. The sighting lasted 4 or 5 minutes, at a distance of 300 to 350 yards, and "we didn't want to get any closer". He was uncertain about the colour, perhaps greenish grey. There were two humps, as thick as a man's thigh, say 200 mm (8 inches). The head was not much bigger than the body, but he could not see much detail. The length of the head and two humps would have come to 9 or 10 feet [3 metres].

Third Witness. John Willett, aged 55, Mick's son-in-law. He provided a quite different account of the circumstances. It was at least 35 years before. He said that the sighting occurred in the afternoon, and that they were halfway across the bay, and had decided to head home because the weather had turned rough and windy, with light rain. He contested the statements of the other two, and said he distinctly remembered putting his head down against the wind, and also remembered the sea being choppy. The animal appeared only 20 or 30 feet away [6 or 9 metres]. I asked him twice. He was sure it was close because the water was bad. The sighting lasted 1½ to 2 minutes, and they were scared. He mentioned that the animal was moving parallel to them, but in the opposite direction ie north. The motor had probably disturbed it.

He distinctly remembered three humps, and possibly four, and they were quite distinct despite the very rough water. They were at least a foot in diameter, the distance along the tops of each hump being about 5 or 6 feet [150 or 180 cm], and the space between the humps 3 or 4 feet [say a metre], making a total length of 20 to 30 feet [6 to 9 metres]. He couldn't remember the colour. However, he did say the head was like a snake's or eel's and, whereas the other two failed to see any tail, he volunteered, without being asked, that he saw the tail come out of the water just before the animal submerged. It was like a very large paddle, flat and horizontal - unlike a fish's vertical tail - and was not forked. He described its motion as like a snake sliding over three rocks. The body itself did not move up and down i.e. there were no coils, but the humps moved with a fluid motion.

Comments. After such a lapse of time, the variations in the accounts are not surprising. Indeed, this makes them all the more valuable, by demonstrating that the witnesses' memories have not been altered by telling and retelling the story among themselves. As far as the circumstances of the sighting, I am inclined to put more credence on the third witness. The other two were probably recalling the weather at the start of the excursion. Also, although he has probably underestimated the distance, his estimate of the duration of the sighting is probably more accurate, seeing that the animal did not apparently get too far away. Besides, you can see a lot in 1½ to 2 minutes, if your adrenaline is pumping. In any case, it is clear that the three descriptions are all variations on a theme.

When did it take place? Unless a witness has some circumstance or event to "anchor" a sighting, it is very difficult to remember exactly when a sighting took place. Therefore, I am more inclined to accept the estimate of Peter, who was just a young boy at the time. While the lives of adults tend to be routine, those of children are constantly changing with respect to school and social life. So if Peter said he was 10 or 11, it is unlikely he was as young as 7 or 8, or as old as 14 or 15. Taken at face value, this would place the unreported sighting about 1958 or 1959 - just before the much better publicised Deception Bay "monster" of 1959-60. I find that amazing! Not only that, it appears to have been a different kind of animal.

11. The Great Tasmanian Globster Expeditions

For the better part of two weeks in March 1962 the front pages of the Tasmanian press went hot with the news of scientific expeditions to a remote beach on the west of Tasmania to examine a mysterious blob lying there. At the time, the only name applied to it was "monster", but the American zoologist/journalist, Ivan Sanderson christened it the "globster", and the term has stuck for not only this object, but others which randomly turn up around the world.[151]

The story actually began in August 1960, when Don Fenton and two of his stockmen, Jack Boote and Ray Anthony were rounding up cattle, and came across it about three kilometres north of the Interview River, south of Sandy Cape. In their estimation, it measured 20 feet [6.1 metres] long, 18 feet [5.5 metres] wide, and 4½ feet [1.4 metres] high, and weighed 5 to 10 tons, though how they estimated that is hard to say. They talked about it to a few people, and after nearly two years, it came to the attention of G. C. Cramp, a businessman and naturalist of Hobart. After discussions with the Tasmanian Museum, he financed an aerial search, and once it was located, a scientific team was set up, consisting of two members of the C.S.I.R.O., Bruce Mollison and Max Bennett, and two members of the Tasmanian Field Naturalists Club, L. E. Wall and J. A. Lewis. Departing on 2 March 1962, they hiked over the rugged terrain of the west coast, arriving at the blob five days later. Remember, this was long before the age of mobile phones, but they still managed to telephone Mr Cramp and inform him that it was something entirely new and unknown. At that, the fat hit the fire.[152]

> The party described it in general outline as like a huge turtle, without appendages. It was initially covered with fine hair, described by stockmen as being like sheep's wool, with a greasy feel. They likened it to a three month's coat of a Border Leicester. The animal had a hump of about four feet in front and tapered gradually to about six inches [15 cm] to what they presumed to be the back.[153]

It also possessed no obvious eyes, head, or bony structure. However, it did have what appeared to be hairless slits resembling gills on either side of the fore section, with four large, overhanging lobes in front, and between the centre pair, a smooth, gullet-like orifice. On the rear margins were cushion like protrusions about 2 feet [60 cm] wide and 18 inches [45 cm] deep, each with a single row of spines, sharp and hard, thick as a pencil, and gill like. The dogs and horses kept their distance, because it smelled like strong battery acid. The party made an incision in the high part, and discovered the resilient flesh was composed of numerous tendon like threads welded together with a fatty substance. This was weird, with a capital W.

The next day speculation was rife as to its possible identity.[154] Perhaps it was a giant devil ray, with can be 6 metres across, with the mouth buried in the sand - or maybe a whale shark. Photos were published, which at least revealed that, if it were 4½ feet high, then much of it was buried in the sand. A couple of days later, Prof. A. M. Clark of the University of Tasmania did suggest that it might be a huge ray, and that the dried out small bristles might look like clipped wool.[155]

At this point a Mr. R. H. Timberly of Mosman Park, Perth added his two cents' worth.[156] Back in 1934, he and his father had discovered something similar washed ashore at Henrietta Rocks, Rottnest Island, and he produced photographs and newspaper clippings to prove it. It had also been a seven day wonder. It had been similar in appearance, 18 feet long, roughly stingray shaped, with a long tail and vaguely formed flippers. It was believed to have possessed a toothless mouth and frontal bones, but it was also covered with a wool-like coat. Its cream coloured flesh had the consistency of tough tripe.

The team had reported that only two possibilities existed: that it was an unknown animal, or the remnant of a known animal - something which one would have thought to have been fairly obvious. Questions were asked in Parliament, and a new scientific team was established, consisting of Drs. John Calaby, A. M. Olsen, Eric R.Guiler, and W. Bryden, zoologists whom, when I attended university a decade later, I revered as some of the big names in the field. They flew out by helicopter, and returned two days ahead of schedule.[157]

It was on 19 March that their report was produced.[158] The globster had obviously decayed and shrunk in the two years since it had been first discovered, for the exposed portion measured 6 feet long and 2 feet wide [180 x 60 cm]. Having dug around it, passed a rope under it, and pulled it out, they discovered that the full size was 8 foot by 3 foot, and it was 10 inches [25 cm] deep. However, the original size was still visible when it was found that, a few inches below the surface was a layer of sand stained black by organic material, which extended 8 feet on the north side, none on the southern side, and 18 feet on the seaward side, following the natural slope of the beach. Its weight was estimated at a few hundred pounds.

It consisted of "tough material loaded with fatty or oily substances", which gave off a strange, rancid smell of higher fatty acids, a smell also present in the stained sand. No bones, spines, or other hard structures were present, and "[t]he hairlike material on the exposed surfaces was merely a consequence of desiccation and leaching of fat-filled fibrous material." They decided it was "a decomposing portion of a large marine animal" - something nobody had ever doubted - but it was "not inconsistent with blubber."

Do you believe in coincidences? Yet another globster was washed up in the same general area in late 1970, this time about 50 km south of Temna, and it was discovered by the same man, Don Fenton, with his stockmen. This time, a report from the Burnie *Advocate*, Kerry Pink, accompanied with photographer, Don Carter flew in on a Cessna, complete with a trail bike on the back. A humped blob about 10 feet by 4 feet [3 x 1.2 metres] with the appearance and smell of rotting whale, and a hide like leather, met their eyes (and noses). It was decorated with the same wool-like growths as the 1962 globster.[159] This time, the Government and the scientific community took no notice whatsoever.

Science, however, marches on. Over the years a number of such "globsters" have found their way onto the beaches throughout the world, and we now know a little more about them. In 1965 one turned up on Muriwai Beach in New Zealand, where it was discovered by a Marine Department officer. It was 30 feet [9 metres] long and 8 feet [2½ metres] high, and described as possessing a hide a quarter of an inch [6 mm] thick, under was a layer of fat, then solid meat. Hair four to six inches [10 to 15 cm] long covered its length and, when washed clean, had a soft, wooley texture.

Alas! Miss J. Robb, a Senior Lecturer in Zoology at Auckland University, brought the subject down to earth. The "hair" was really long strands of fibrous material, all that remained of the outermost few centimetres of blubber. The "globster" was the remnant of a dead whale![160]

Early in this century, an international team of scientists examined samples of a number of globsters, including the first Tasmanian one, and conclusively proved that they were the remains of whale blubber.[161] Bit of an anticlimax, wasn't it! But at least the remains of the Tasmanian globster, hacked off with an axe during the first expedition, are on display at the Tasmanian Museum.

It seems the age of the globster is still not over. In 1998 another one was discovered at Sundown Point, south of the Arthur River in Tasmania. It was also determined to be a blob of blubber.[162]

12. The Last (Recorded) Visitors to the East Coast

[83] The war did not completely eclipse interest in sea serpents. On Wednesday, 5 November 1941 a Brisbane man, J. G. Barnes was out fishing with a friend off Mooloolabah when "a huge serpentine creature appeared on the surface of the water about a quarter of a mile [400 metres] distant."[163] He estimated it was 60 feet [18 metres] long, but its most striking feature was what looked like a red beard.

And that was what gave it away. Dr. T. Marshall, the Queensland Museum ichthyologist, immediately recognized it as "a huge ribbon fish" or, as we would now call it, the giant oarfish, *Regalecus glesne*, which bears a long red dorsal fin down the length of its body, and a red crest on its head. Since they seldom grow beyond 20 or 30 feet [6 or 9 metres] in length, Dr Marshall suggested they had witnessed something very unusual: two oarfish swimming in tandem, but I consider it more likely that the distance involved simply led them to overestimate its length.

[84] After that, a long hiatus intervened - at least on the east coast, until the early 1960s, as described in Chapter 10. But in 1964 came something really special: close-up, coloured photographs. (Well, maybe.) In 1960, a Breton photographer, Robert le Serrec had left France with his family aboard his yawl, the *Saint-Yves d'Armor*, only to be wrecked near Mackay. After purchasing an 18 foot [5½ m] motor launch, he went off to spend three months on Hook Island with his wife, Raymonde, his children, and a Sydney skindiver called Henk de Jong. Hook Island is one of the Whitsunday Islands in the Barrier Reef, and right next to the popular tourist resort of Hayman Island. Significantly or otherwise, this means it was not far from where Boyd Lee claimed to have seen the huge turtle eating monster [47] in 1932. Let us now take up the story as le Serrec told it.[164]

They were anchored in one of the inlets called Stonehaven Bay, where they had been kept under canvas for four days by a storm. However, on 12 December the sky was again clear and the sea calm, so about 9 o'clock they decided to cross the bay to wash their clothes in a waterfall. It was not long after they had left the beach that Raymonde drew their attention to a strange object in the water. It appeared to be an enormous head attached to a supple body 70 feet [21 m] long. They slowed the engine, got out their cameras, and slowly began to circle the monster. Le Serrec admitted to being scared, because even a clumsy move by the animal would have smashed their launch to pieces.

As the children started getting scared as well, the three adults took them back to camp before returning to examine the creature. They could see two little whitish eyes peering up at them. Henk got into the dinghy, and they began filming him. As the monster still did not move, it was decided that both le Serrec and de Jong would go underwater and do their filming close up, de Jong armed with a powerhead loaded with a 12-gauge cartridge, designed to be used against sharks, but of dubious benefit against something of this size. Just the same, the water was murky, and it was not until they got to within 6 metres that they could see the head clearly.

At first they thought the monster might be dead, for it was lying motionless on the sandy bottom, and bore a wound about five feet [1½ metres] long, which seemed to reach to the spine, and to have been torn by teeth or a propeller. The head was about four feet [1.2 metres] from top to bottom, and the jaws four feet wide, with a fragment of some darkish material - perhaps a fish - hanging from the upper jaw. The lower jaw was flat, the teeth small, and the interior of the mouth whitish (an unusual colour!). They noted that, behind the head, the body was about 2ft. 4 in. [71 cm] thick (one wonders how he could have been so precise), and continued that way for about 25 ft. [7.6 m], after which it tapered off to a whiplike tail.

The general color of the body was black with 1ft. [30 cm] - wide brownish rings every 5 ft. [1½ m] - the first starting just behind the head.

The skin was smooth and dull.

Fig. 11A.   Robert le Serrec's photo of the monster.
The original was in colour.

Fins and spines were both absent, and they failed to notice any nostrils, although they felt sure they must have been present.

When le Serrec started the camera, to their shock, the head rose from the bottom and turned towards them, it mouth opening several times. They swam frantically back to the boat, where they found Raymonde had been so upset, she had stalled the motor. She told them her impression was that the monster was moving with less than its normal vigour and ease, twisting sideways and seeming to drag itself instead of moving naturally. Just the same, by the time they had got the engine running, the monster had disappeared, and despite their searches over the following few days, it was never seen again.

The motion film was too blurred to be of any use, but he did obtain some good still shots, as you can see. Le Serrec waited a couple of months until they were developed before releasing the story. At that point, when he attempted to sell the photos in the Unites States, a zoological writer, Ivan Sanderson was asked to check them out. Sanderson and Heuvelmans were friends and collaborators, for both were intensely interested in cryptozoology, the search for unknown animals, and suddenly they were communicating by trans-Atlantic telephone. They were not impressed. In their opinion, it could have been a simply a huge roll of cloth or plastic dumped in the water, or possibly some sort of wreckage discovered there and altered to resemble a sea monster.[165]

Heuvelmans was also suspicious of the way the children had been moved out of the way; perhaps he was afraid they'd spill the beans. He also thought it strange that the men should be prepared to swim up close to it when they had been afraid it might destroy the boat. From a zoological perspective, it did not seem right that the eyes were pointing upwards, as that occurs only in some bottom dwelling fish. For myself, I find it strange that it possessed no fins or flippers with which to stabilise it in the water. Some commentators have likened it to a giant tadpole, but tadpoles possess vertical fins along both the top and bottom of their tails. It should better be described as a colossal sperm.

Then we learn that, on returning to France, he was arrested and sentenced to six months' imprisonment because he had left the country while his ship was still "attached" ie its supplies had not been paid for. Then it transpired that, in 1959 ie the year before he departed, he had encouraged some young men to sail with him provided they "share the expenses" of what was to have been a financial venture, and that he had taken the expenses and left them behind. Tellingly, he had told them: "I have another thing in reserve which will bring in a lot of money … it is to do with the sea serpent."

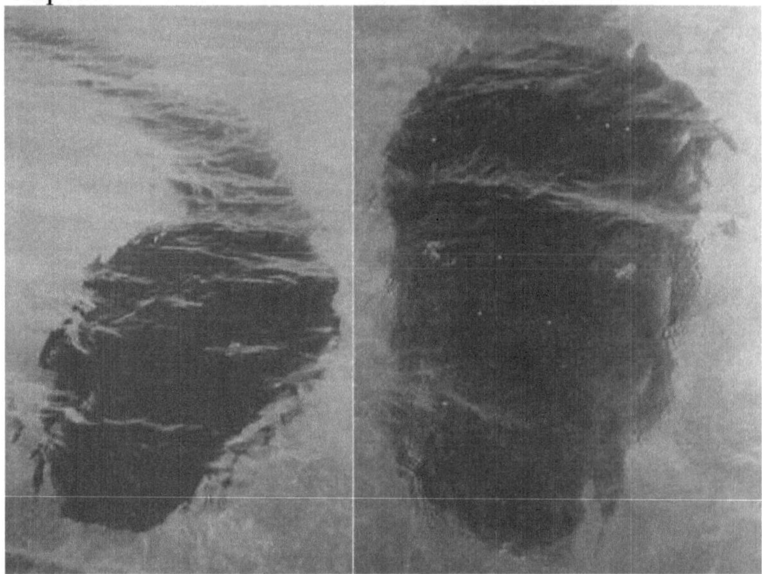
Fig. 11B. Close up of the head

Darren Naish, a zoology blogger with a sceptical, but open minded interest in cryptozoology, has also pointed out that the close up photographs of the head reveal areas at the bottom where the edges are overlapped with sand, exactly what you would expect if someone had placed handfuls of sand there to weight down a roll of plastic.[166]

Finally, whenever the authenticity of a story is in doubt, we need to ask the question: has anything similar been reported elsewhere? In this case, the answer is no. Dr Heuvelmans has recorded 349 plausible sea serpent sightings, and many others have been uncovered since, but there was no colossal sperm anywhere among them.

No, much as I like the Hook Island monster, and would like it to be true, I'm afraid it doesn't add up.

[85] You will remember that, in 1935 a man saw a leopard seal at Aireys Inlet, Victoria, and thought it was a sea serpent [63]. In 1973 two men were fishing in the same area when something a bit more mysterious popped up briefly in front of them. It was reported in the press at the time, and both witnesses independently provided me with written accounts in 1987.[167]

The witnesses were architect Neil Blyth, 25 and his then father-in-law, Norman Robertson. About half past three on the dull winter's day of Sunday 3 June 1973, they launched their boat from Aireys Inlet and headed south, past Eastern view, and settled down to fish about a kilometre off shore. A large swell ie waves four to five feet [1.2 to 1.5 metres] high, was running, but without white caps, except at the beach itself. When a swell rears towards breaking point, a hissing sound is quite audible, so when Mr Robertson heard a hissing sound he assumed that an unusually large swell was approaching the boat. He looked up, only to see, not any variation in the waves, but a strange object rise out of the water perhaps 60 yards away.

It was a long, thin neck, graceful, with a slight S-bend, appearing black and shiny and in silhouette against the dull light. At first, Robertson thought it might have been the tail of a whale, but then they both noticed a blob on the end which was obviously a head. Perhaps due to the dull light, they were unable to notice any details, such as eyes. The vision lasted only about three seconds, and then, instead of diving, it simply slid back into the water in the same diagonal direction in which it had risen.

Once back on shore, they both drew sketches of what they had seen, after which Robertson called the *Geelong Advertiser*. Not unexpectedly, their interpretations differ slightly. Robertson drew a rather squarish head, while Blyth saw it as more pointed. ("Dog-like" was how it was cited in the press, but he wasn't prepared to confirm that.) Blyth felt that it stood out at about 60 degrees from the surface, while Robertson opted for closer to the perpendicular.

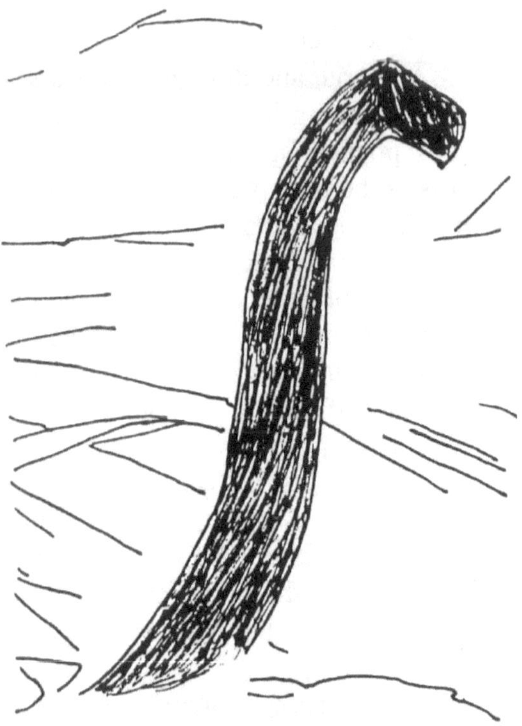

Fig. 12. Norman Robertson's contemporary sketch.

Obviously, in such a brief observation, estimating size would have been a rather hit and miss affair. Robertson estimated its height as 9 feet [2.7 metres] and thickness as 12 inches [30 cm], while Blyth's estimates were 6 feet and 9 inches respectively. However, Robertson thought the distance was greater so, as he put it, "it rather cancels out".

Mr Robertson provided me with some information which had not been reported at the time. About two hours before their sighting, a woman at the Aireys Inlet store, about 400 yards from the beach, observed an unusual dark object moving along the surface of the water parallel to the shore line in the direction of Eastern View. Also, about the same time, Mr Robertson's wife noticed a large number of fish tossing themselves onto the beach at Aireys Inlet.

[86] By 2002, word had got around my workplace that I was interested in mystery animals, so one of my colleagues, Toni Womal approached me about an experience she had had as a little girl.

Our interview took place on 8 August 2002, but the events in question occurred when she was about ten years old, so it was probably 1974, during the summer school holidays ie about January. The presence of a king tide may help to localise it further in time.

At the time, she was living at Bowen, North Queensland, and went to the seaside with her eight-year-old brother, Stephen and her grandfather, Les Womal, now deceased. They had gone out to a rock, known locally as Womal's Rock, about 100 metres off shore, and while Grandpa was fishing from the rock, the two children amused themselves in a rock pool. It was only about 9 o'clock in the morning, so the weather was still a bit cool, although the day was fine, and would later turn hot. There was a king tide, and the water was choppy. Suddenly, their grandfather, without uttering a word, beckoned to them to come out of the water and stand beside him. He then gestured towards a creature about 100 metres further out. The sighting probably lasted only a few seconds, but it was very vivid. They were all mortally afraid of snakes, so they stayed on the rock all day, until the tide went out, and was about to turn. Then, their grandfather announced: "Get changed; we're going home", and he carried them back to shore. He didn't mention the animal again.

What was it like? After all these years, it was hard for her to provide more than an impression, but it was essentially a series of vertical undulations. The creature was very wide - perhaps a metre thick - but certainly, its body was bigger than that of their grandfather, who was "a big Island man" (Toni is of Kanaka descent). It was glistening, shiny black, and rolling like a python. The head was not visible, and it just disappeared. She was unable to be precise about the number of undulations.

So what was it? Sceptics will have legitimate reservations, considering the brevity of the sighting, the youth of the witness, and the lapse of years. Against this, however, one must put the extreme fear reaction of the mature man accompanying them. No matter how much we pare it with Occam's razor, we are still left with something very big, elongated, and undulating. No fish sticks out as meeting that description. Sea snakes are much, much smaller. And, if her memory is correct that the undulations were vertical, this could only refer to a mammal. Readers will also no doubt be aware that reports of similar elongated, vertically undulating "sea serpents" have been received from all corners of the oceans.

Considering that this story came to light only because of my close contact with the witness, one wonders how many other such stories are "out there".

[87] Reports seem to come in about once a decade. In the 1980s, of course, there was the Bynoe Harbour case (chapter 9). Then, in 1995, something turned up in southeast Queensland, in a deep inlet halfway between Bundaberg and Maryborough, formed when the Burrum and Isis Rivers unite at about 25° 13' S, 153° 33' E - in fact, very close to the village of Buxton. The two fishermen involved were so scared of ridicule, they did not dare to even show their faces, let alone leave their names. Instead, an unsigned letter with the accompanying drawing was slipped under the door of the office of the weekly *Isis Town & Country* newspaper in Childers.

During the first week of September a friend and myself were fishing from a tinnie.

It was about three in the afternoon and we were near the junction of the Isis and Burrum Rivers, when I spotted something unusual.

I called my companion's attention to it and for what seemed about a minute we watched what appeared to be an enormous snake with a bulbous head. I really do mean enormous the neck/body was upright out of the water and was topped by a head the size of a Labrador dog, while the neck seemed about half the girth of a timber power pole.

It was very dark grey, almost black and neither of us noticed any teeth, tongue, ears, fur or scales. There did seem to be a small wash as it moved slowly upstream but neither of us became aware of any swimming motion.

After a while it just slipped under the water and that was it, we didn't see it again. It definitely did not dive, it slid away.

And that, folks, is the most recent sighting in my records. However, if the witnesses' reluctance to be identified is any indication of a general trend, I suspect that more than one sighting has gone unreported in the past quarter century.

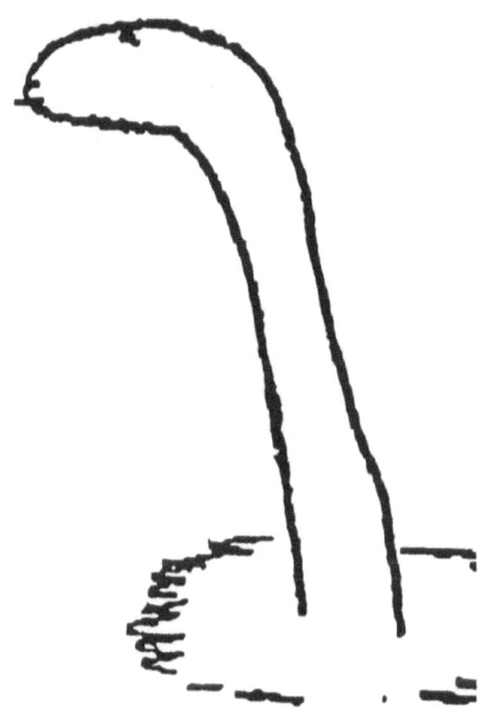

Fig. 13. Anonymous sketch of the Burrum Heads monster

13. Loose Ends

Sea serpents are such a controversial subject, and since the information on them is scattered throughout many different publications, it is important to place a last few loose ends on record.

Anybody investigating mystery animals in Australia will, sooner or later, cross paths with an eccentric character named Rex Gilroy, who for fifty years or so has been researching such animals, as well as a host of other, allegedly anomalous subjects.[168] He used to run a private museum on this basis. Regrettably, he does not co-operate with other researchers. You can ask for the documentation of any sighting he reports, but it will never be forthcoming. Not only is he uncritical, but he is constantly coming up with material which no other researcher has ever heard about.

For example, he believes that *Megalania prisca*, a goanna 6 metres long, which may have still been around when the first Aborigines arrived, is still extant in many parts of the country, and he cites alleged witnesses of goannas even larger: 9 metres or 15 metres. One would think they would be highly visible, due to their need to sunbathe to reach a working body temperature, and that they would be fearfully dangerous predators. Nevertheless, he is the only researcher who claims to have found witnesses. I was able to locate one of them, and she denied every word. Paul Cropper, who has been following up reports of mystery animals for most of his adult life, told me that he has never even heard a bad hoax of a giant goanna.

I don't know where he gets these stories, but in his 1995 book, *Mysterious Australia*, and later publications, he introduces even more fanciful accounts: of a monster in an outback Queensland lake never more than two metres deep, of a (relatively) small sauropod dinosaur in a swamp near Singleton, New South Wales, and of a monstrous tyrannosaur-like flesh-eating dinosaur in northern Australia.

While it would be tempting to write Gilroy off, nevertheless, as a media personality and the manager of a private museum, he manages to flush out witnesses to genuine anomalous animals. He was also the first person to publicise the yowie, Australia's answer to bigfoot, something I first considered ridiculous until lots of independent reports started coming in.[169] Personally, I am not prepared to accept anything Rex Gilroy says without independent corroboration - but I am not prepared to reject everything either.

The reason I say this is because he devotes a whole chapter of *Mysterious Australia*[170] to sea serpents in the Hawkesbury River, New South Wales. Featured are many reports of the familiar long neck sticking out of the water, some with two humps (occasionally reported elsewhere), and a few with a pair of paddles in front (less commonly reported). He identifies them as plesiosaurs. Included also are more fanciful stories, such as the overturning of boats, and the snatching of cattle off the shore in broad daylight.

Locating his alleged witnesses was next to impossible, because of the the great frequency of people with the same surname and initial, and the fact that they might have lived outside the area of the sighting, or have left their previous address. Nevertheless, I was able to find one witness with an unusual name: Michael Rousek (pronounced *roo*-seck), whose story was recorded on pages 162-3. It took place in March 1978, and Rex Gilroy interviewed him the following year. He was manning the river-bank pumps on a property north of Penrith, which would make it a good distance from the sea. He claimed that the river was both very deep and very wide at that point. It was about 2 p.m. when out of the water rose a dark brown body, the visible section being estimated at 10 feet long by 6 feet wide [3 x 1.8 metres], and the humps about 2 foot 6 inches [76 cm] above the water level. He called over his partner, Jim Comack and two other men cutting turf, and they all saw it.

I was able to speak to Mr Rousek about 1996.

He sounded elderly, and his memory was probably not the best, so I had to pry the information out of him. (His accent also did not help.) However, he readily admitted to the experience. He had been cutting turf at a farm "a good ten years ago" when the object rose out of the depths. It was just after lunch and the day was clear. The object was about 50 yards away, and was visible for about 5 minutes. It was just one large body, and was a dark colour. When I asked if it swam upstream or downstream, he said it just rose up, producing a big wave, and then went down again. He also gave the name of the other witness as Jim O'Comack, but I wasn't able to locate him under either name.

This is slightly different from Gilroy's account, but since the latter interviewed him just a year after the event, I am prepared to trust it. I wish I could say the same for all his stories.

At the time of the Aireys Inlet sighting in 1973, some journalists made reference to an earlier encounter at Gabo Island. You will remember that this stretch of coast produced many sightings in the early years, but this one appears to have been in the late 1960s or very early 1970s - a time later than Trove's digitalised newspapers. The journalist responsible seems to have been Graham Perkin, the editor for *The Age* (Melbourne) from 1966 to 1975.[171]

Perkin was an expert of the "beat up": the sort of story which titillated the reader's imagination without being an actual invention. In this case, he cultivated the friendship of the keeper of the Gabo Island lighthouse, who told of nocturnal apparitions which might have been a whale, a sea serpent, or a Soviet submarine. That last reference suggests that we are dealing with the typical long neck protruding periscope-like from the surface, but only the discovery of the original article can confirm it.

The late Peter Chapple, of Rare Fauna Research in Victoria, obtained a sea serpent report and, since his organisation dealt with big cats and thylacines, he gracious mailed the document to me. Regrettably, I never saw it; it was lost in the mail - and there was no back-up copy.

A media personality, Tim Bull ("Tim the Yowie Man") claimed to have received a sea serpent report , but when I requested a copy, he informed me it had been mislaid. Nevertheless, I have reason to believe that it is the following story.[172] It was published in 2000 and concerns a person named Herbert, who claimed to have twice seen a sea serpent while fishing near Rottnest Island, off-shore from Perth. On the first occasion he was one of a party of four, the second time, a few years later, he was by himself.

"It was like a whirlpool, swimming around in a big feeding frenzy before it disappeared," he says. "The second time, it actually poked its tiny head out of the water. It was a slimy greenish-blackish colour, about 13 metres long. It had four webbed feet, two on each side, and looked like it could walk on land. I thought of jumping in and catching it, but then it took off."

If he was prepared to grab a 13 metre monster, even one with a tiny head, he is a braver, or more foolish man than I am. Anyway, it is not often that four feet (? flippers) are seen.

For the sake of completeness, I might as well include two reports from Papua New Guinea, because you won't read them elsewhere. The first one comes from *The ABC Weekly* of 31 July 1943, and it references Hall Sound which, with the adjacent Yule Island, lies approximately 100 km northwest in a straight line from Port Moresby.

It is over twenty years now since Monsignor Verjus, the Catholic Archbishop of Papua, sitting on his verandah and piously saying his prayers, saw in the waters of Hall Sound an amazing phenomenon: nothing less than the sea-serpent of legend and fame.

The Archbishop, very old, very pious, and little concerned with the things of this world (he died not long after), did not trouble himself to do anything about it. He saw a huge body lashing the waters of the Sound, something incredibly long, with a great head that was afterwards described as being "like a very big horse's head," but as it did not seem to be doing any harm, and as it shortly went down and did not come back, he simply went on with his prayers.

Not so the Mission Sisters, who were on the shore with a number of the native children. They were terrified of the sight; they gathered their charges together and ran back to the house as fast as they could. Natives near the shore were also badly frightened and ran away. The serpent went down presently, and was not seen again. But the archbishop and the sisters, and innumerable Papuans, were quite sure they had seen it.[173]

Now, I have a few problems with this, notably the date. The author implies it took place some time around 1920. However, except for the unlikely event that there was a second bishop at Yule Island coincidentally named Verjus, the witness could only have been Henri Stanislas Verjus[174], who arrived at Yule Island in 1885, was consecrated bishop there in 1889, and departed in 1892 before passing away in Italy the same year. It is true that he was "very pious", because he has been declared Venerable ie he is on the way to being made a saint, but, far from being "little concerned with the things of this world", he had been an active explorer. Nor was he "very old"; he died at the age of only 32½, worn out by the rigours of the tropical climate. Also, although he was consecrated bishop, he does not appear to have ever been created archbishop.

One wonders, therefore, where the author got his or her information, and whether there are any further errors lurking in there undetected.

The second PNG case relates to New Ireland, and in particular, a tiny inlet called Ramat Bay at 3° 35' S, 152° 22' E. On the hill overlooking it stood - at least during the period in question - a plantation house owned by Bernie Gash, an expatriate Englishman who lived in Namatanai and operated a coconut plantation. In July 1983 he and his indigenous wife were interviewed by J. Richard Greenwell, the secretary of the International Society of Cryptozoology, which acted as a zoological forum for the investigation of unknown animals. This is what they told him.[175]

In August 1958, about 9.30 or 10 in the morning, a creature came into the bay to within a few hundred feet of the shore, turned, and moved out again, being visible for three or four minutes. Its speed was estimated at five to six knots [9 - 11 kph], and its length about 50 feet [15¼ metres]. The latter consisted of four grey-green loops about 10 feet apart without any space between the loops, and there was a "frill" along its back. They did not see any head, but did notice a vertical, segmented tail about two feet [60 cm] long.

Both husband and wife were interviewed separately about the second incident, because the whole family had been present. About 5 p.m. on 26 April 1981, at a distance of 200 to 300 yards, there appeared a neck 10 to 15 feet [3 to 4½ metres] long and two feet [60 cm] wide, surmounted by a head like a python's. The distance and the fading light converted it into a black silhouette, which they watched for two or three minutes until it splashed down and submerged. Three minutes later, however, it reappeared as a series of three small loops (the drawing shows four) rolling along until it sank.

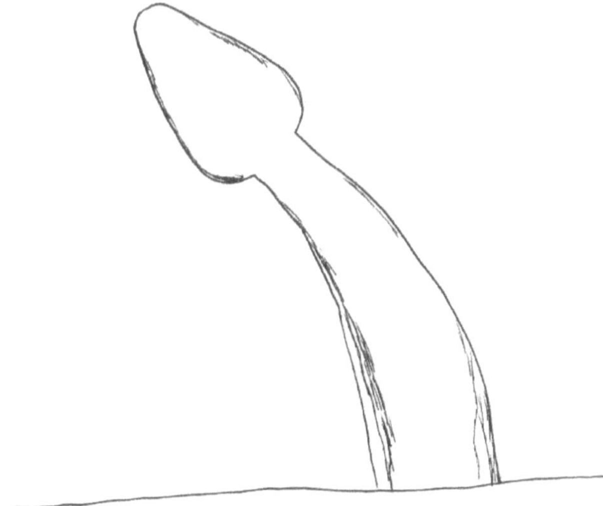

Fig. 14A. Bernie Gash's sketch of the 1981 appearance in Ramat Bay.

Fig. 14B. Second appearance three minutes later.

Mr Gash's 11-year-old son, Edward was said to have observed the animal seven times in the period 1981-82, probably because he lived in the house overlooking the bay itself.

With the aid of anthropologist, Roy Wagner, Mr Greenwell interviewed twelve Barok tribesmen at the village of Kolanabai. They claimed that they often encountered it far out at sea on both sides of the narrow island when fishing, and called it *a-in-milo* (pronounced "ah-een-millaw"), or "fish eel". They told him it was dark in colour, and undulated vertically. Of course, two sightings separated by 23 years should not automatically be assumed to refer to the same species, but a continuing tradition among the indigenous population would tip the scales in favour of that interpretation.

The final encounter has nothing to do with Australia, except the nationality of the witness. Nevertheless, I feel it should be placed on record for future researchers to ponder.

In the first week of 2003, I was lying in bed at night, when I received a phone call from a Mr Mike Cleary, who was seeking specific information on Australian cryptids for the husband of his niece in the UK. Unfortunately, I was not able to help him. Then he told me an incredible story.

He has been a diver for more than 35 years. About 10 years or so beforehand he was in a diving bell with a companion off the south-east coast of Japan, checking bottom sites for an oil rig. They were at a depth of 1,700 feet [> 500 metres] when an unknown creature approached the bell and circled it.

It was about 25 foot [7½ m] long. It had no visible scales, and the skin changed colour in the light from the bell (which, I gather, is a common occurrence at this depth). It swam with horizontal undulations, and possessed just a single, elongated dorsal fin, extending down the body. I got the impression that it was like an eel's. He couldn't say much about the tail, but didn't think there was a tail fluke.

The head was like a sea horse's, the eyes like a cow's, and teeth like a barracuda's.

No constriction existed between the neck and body, but one ran into the other. However, 8 feet [2½ m] from the front was a pair a limbs, about 4 feet long. There was also a pair of hind limbs. I questioned him about this in particular, but he was emphatic that these were not fins, but webbed limbs.

What sort of creature could this be? The elongated dorsal fin and the horizontal undulations mean it had to be some sort of fish – but what? The obvious choice is some very large eel, or elongated shark – although none, to my knowledge, are of such a size. At a pinch, it might even have been an oarfish. However, it is the limbs that are the real problem. As you are no doubt aware, the vast majority of fish, the teleosts, possess rayed fins, which could hardly be mistaken for limbs, or even paddles. The largest fishes tend to be sharks, but their fins are also hard to mistake for limbs, and most people – especially divers – would be familiar with them. But there once existed a vast array of lobe-finned fish, of which only a few relic species are now known to exist. One group is the Dipnoi, or lungfishes, and the other is the Crossopterygians, whose lobed fins evolved into the legs which all land vertebrates now walk on. However, except for the two species of coelacanth, they all went extinct about the same time as the dinosaurs, and were on the way out for a long, long time before that.

So, if Mr Cleary's perception and memory were accurate, something very strange was swimming around off the coast of Japan.

14. So What Are They?

So now you have the evidence. Before you read this book, I bet you never imagined the extent of the phenomenon. Leaving out the big fish, globsters, and loose ends, we are left with 87 reports. Some bear all the signs of a hoax, some can be reasonably provided with a conventional explanation, and some are too brief or ambiguous to be useful. However, if we exclude these, we are still left with 60 which are worthy of consideration. Are there any frauds or misidentifications lurking among them? Almost certainly. But all 60? I don't think so. And remember: if only one of them is genuine, then we are looking at a large animal new to science.

Are you sceptical? I should hope so. That is the proper attitude of science. It doesn't mean debunking, or rejecting a thesis on principle, but rather, critically examining the evidence, and not taking a stated position for granted. You will have noticed, for example, how I have been careful to deconstruct the various reports, not only to seek a conventional explanation, but also to determine whether particular details may be in error.

Of course, a hard line sceptic will complain that the evidence is all anecdotal. Well, anecdotal evidence puts people in jail, because in law, anecdotal evidence is called "eyewitness testimony". It even applies to science. Not all science takes place in a laboratory, and can be replicated. Quite often, especially in the areas of wildlife zoology, meteorology, or astronomy, a scientist witnesses something ephemeral, and unlikely to be repeated, at least not on demand. In such cases, the anecdote is called "direct observation", and is held in high regard. Admittedly, it is usually recorded shortly after the event, but the same applies to many of the newspaper articles you'd just read. Furthermore, in wildlife papers we also occasionally see the words: "There are anecdotal evidence that …", which is a shorthand way of saying: "I didn't see it myself, but I heard it from people who sounded reliable."

So let's not reject eyewitness testimony offhand. It is not perfect, but the administration of justice would collapse if it were completely unreliable. The law has developed methods of dealing with its shortfalls, which are well known. With dramatic events, laden with emotion, such as crimes and amazing animals, the witnesses focus on the details which are important to them, often distorting them, and interpreting them according to their own presuppositions. These do not necessarily concur with those relevant to a second witness. They also seldom attempt to dispassionately observe every detail. I have already mentioned the difficulties involved in estimating distance and size, and the tendency for fear and shock to produce exaggeration.

Then there is memory. No doubt you have had the experience of seeing a picture or listening to a song after a significant lapse of time, and discovering that it was not exactly how you remembered it. The human brain is not a computer. Whenever you recall a scene, your brain has to reconstruct it again from the elements somehow recorded in its cells. Each time it does it, it not only refreshes the memory and consolidates it, but there is also the opportunity for it to be distorted. Often, the details coalesce into what you think you should have seen. If two witnesses discuss the episode, they will tend to contaminate each other's memory.

Then there is simply the fact that some people make better witnesses than others. Once I interviewed separately two women who had witnessed a strange cat-like animal in central Queensland. Their memories were so divergent, they were next to worthless. Yet if I had interviewed only one, I would have assumed it was reliable. On the other hand, I also interviewed two male witnesses for another event. This time, however, their memories lined up except for one detail, *and* they both acknowledged their differences. I regarded them as reliable.[176]

Just the same, we should examine how this plays out in the current field. Take case [82]. Here we had three witnesses who had not compared notes for several decades yet, although their stories were all different, the basic description remained the same. Likewise with the memories of Nigel Tutt and his daughter about the event in Deception Bay [76]. The information provided by Carol was not as detailed as her father's, but the details she supplied were exactly the same, even after 29 years, and without the use of newspaper clippings to refresh her memory. So we shouldn't be too quick to disregard remembered events.

Furthermore, it is the overall picture which counts. Any individual report may be suspect, but a large number cannot be so easily discounted. How many times do people have to report something weird before we accept that something weird is going on?

So what is the overall picture? You cannot have failed to notice the recurring theme of a thin neck and head sticking up, like a periscope, two, three, even as much as six metres above the surface. Half of the animals sighted - 31 in all - fit that description. And this is a minimum, because some reports lack detail, and in some cases, the sea serpent might have simply not lifted its head at all. In a lake or inland waterway you may suspect a tree trunk or a swimming deer, but in the open sea there is *nothing* known which can produce that effect. Not only that, but the reports are independent. Can we imagine that the men who saw an animate periscope in the Burrum inlet in 1995 [case 87] and slipped a letter under the door of the local newspaper, knew anything about the same thing which appeared at Aireys Inlet 22 years before [case 85], or that both groups knew anything about what happened at Cronulla in 1935 [case 65]? Isn't it interesting that, in the first two cases, the animal did not dive, but simply slid back into the water, and that the Townsville sea serpent of 1934 [54] "sank like a submarine" - an unusual detail, wouldn't you say? Not only that, but you will find that similar creatures have been described all over the world. They are the most common type of sea serpent.

This is not to say, of course, that they are all the same. Heuvelmans, in fact, divided them into two types: the "long necked" sea serpent, which has small, often unnoticeable eyes, and the "merhorse", with large eyes and sometimes a mane. Confining ourselves to the Australian cohort, we note that sometimes the head and neck are the only body parts visible, but sometimes the rest of the body comes into view. This itself is nothing more than might be expected. But whereas the visitor to Mourilyan Harbour in 1934 [53] possessed a turtle-like back, the one which came to

Townsville [54] had three humps, covered with scales, and the *Kurumba* sea serpent of 1939 [67] had three humps and a giraffe-like skin pattern which has never been reported elsewhere. The *Dimboola* sea serpent of 1913 [28] possessed at least one hump, and what appears to be a fin or mane, while the one seen by the *Saint-François-Xavier* in1925 [34] had multiple "loops" and a huge fin. I have no explanation for these variations.

So what sort of creatures could they be? Plesiosaurs are most people's immediate response: the famous long-neck marine predators which perished along with the dinosaurs 66 million years ago, when an asteroid hit the earth. Why is something we may ponder. Probably the darkening of the sky by volcanic ash and the burning of vegetation prevented photosynthesis for the basis of the marine food chain, phytoplankton, or plant plankton. When the food chain collapsed, the apex predators dropped off. Nevertheless, I suppose it is theoretically possible for one or two species to have survived.

Superficially, the popular idea of plesiosaurs does match the appearance of the long necked sea serpents. Nevertheless, I have my doubts. First of all, the popular idea is incorrect. The plesiosaur neck permitted little vertical movement. It stuck out in front of the swimming animal, moving side by side. It could not be raised like a swan's the way the old books portrayed it. Secondly, plesiosaurs possessed a relatively squat body, whereas when the long necked sea serpent's body is sighted, it is as often as not elongated, frequently with humps. Take a look at the Figures 5, 7, and 8A on pages 61, 91, and 92. Do they look anything like the popular idea of a plesiosaur?

So what else could they be? Real serpents? It is true that some of them do, indeed, sound like outsized snakes - for example, cases [2], [3], [15], [17], and [75]. On the other hand, the creatures which turned up at Newcastle in 1891 [11] and near Orpheus Island in 1934 [51] sound more like giant eels, for they were endowed with pectoral fins, which no snake possesses. A huge eel sounds more likely than a very large sea snake, so were some of the "snakes" in fact eels, and the fins overlooked?

Just the same, the large body, often with humps, appended to the thin neck would rule out snakes in most cases. Not only that, but when Antoon Oudemans wrote his seminal work, *The Great Sea Serpent* (1892) he noticed something which effectively ruled out any snake: on no occasion was any of them observed to swim by lateral undulations, which is the only way a snake or eel can move. On the contrary, vertical undulations were most often reported. Therefore, they had to be mammals.

All this is first year zoology, but it is useful to explain it here. Imagine a small, worm-like animal wriggling over the mud at the bottom of the primeval seas. Obviously, it is going to wriggle side to side, because it is in a two dimensional world. When it starts swimming, it will naturally do so by lateral undulations. This, essentially, is the ancestry of all the vertebrates, the animals with backbones. All fish possess a bank of muscles down both sides which move the whole body laterally. It is also the reason they possess vertical tail fins. When their descendants climbed onto the land, the tradition was continued. A snake moves on both land and water by flexing its body into lateral loops. If you watch a lizard walking or, more especially, running, you will see that its body also flexes laterally, while its legs are splayed out to the side. Such a limb position, however, is very inefficient, and mammals have improved on it by tucking their legs in under the body. A mammal therefore walks and runs by flexing its spine vertically. For that reason, mammals adapted for swimming, such as the platypus and beaver, have laterally flattened tails and, of course, a whale's tail fluke is horizontal. So, if a sea serpent swims by vertical undulations, it must be a mammal.

Just the same, there are certain mammalian features which must be considered. Firstly, the section of spine attached to the ribs, protecting the lungs, is not very flexible; the spine's main flexibility lies in the lumbar region and tail. A mammal without hind limbs, such as a whale, if it were elongated, would possess a fairly flexible spine, but just the same, it would be unlikely to produce more than two curves when swimming. A series of humps would have to be part of the body, not merely a temporary flexure of the spine.

Secondly, one of the peculiarities of mammals is that they possess only seven cervical (ie neck) vertebrae. Admittedly, there are a few exceptions. Manatees have only six, two-toed sloths five, and three-toed sloths nine. So it is possible for mutations to have a minor effect but, by and large, mammals appear to lack the genetic ability to change the number of their neck vertebrae. Even a giraffe has only seven. To be sure, a giraffe's neck vertebrae are furnished with processes which lock them in place and keep the neck stiff. It would be possible the allow a certain amount of flexibility to such a long neck, but nowhere near as much as (say) a flamingo's, which has seventeen. The manner in which a long neck served the plesiosaurs is a matter of debate, but if the long necked sea serpent is a mammal, it must use its neck in a radically different way. I am inclined to think, therefore, that any description of a neck more than 3 metres long represents either an exaggeration or a misinterpretation. I've frequently mentioned the difficulty of estimating sizes at sea, and a few of the reports mention a neck not only as long as a giraffe's, but as long as a giraffe is high!

If a mammal, then what type? Oudemans suggested a seal, with which I would include sea lions, and many authors have followed him. Now, seals are (relatively) elongated animals, and it is theoretically possible for one to be stretched out until it is serpentine in shape. He also believed the sea serpent had a long tail, even though seals are tailless. Of course, he may be wrong about the tail, but I have other problems with this identification. Firstly, a seal's neck is not very much thinner than its body, and it is far from clear why a huge seal would evolve a long, thin neck. More to the point, seals and sea lions have to return to the land to bear their young. We would therefore have to propose a triple line of evolution: (a) an extra-large, elongated body, (b) a long, thin neck, and (c) the ability to bear and feed its young at sea. That is pushing the limits of probability a bit too far for my liking.

If not a seal, what else? Whales? The most primitive whales, which are supposed to have gone extinct millions of years ago, were the archaeocetes, and one group at least, the Basilosaurids were elongated and eel-like in shape. Even these, of course, had short necks, like any respectable whale, and their skulls were fairly large, but at least they were something like the correct shape, and they could breed at sea. Despite all the problems, they seem the most likely solution.

Perhaps we might examine our data for any reference to the manner of locomotion, or the presence of a tail. And here, it must be admitted that such details were very seldom noticed, or at least mentioned, with respect to those animals with long necks. The thing which allegedly chased Mr Bowman [16] showed a small part of its tail, but it was not described. It was seen to "bend its body in a bow", whatever that means, but its precise method of swimming was not recorded. The *Dimboola* sea serpent [28] was referred to as "undulating", and the sketch implies the undulations were vertical. It also possessed a fish-like tail, although it was not specified whether it was vertical or horizontal. The Townsville monster [54] was motionless, before it simply sank, and later rose, like a submarine. Later witnesses watched it lift its tail several times, and described it as eel-like, without a whale's fluke. The one near Portland Bay in 1935 [59] had a wide tail, like a whale's, with serrations, which it used to thump the water when moving, causing large splashes. When Cecil Walters watched a sea serpent from the *Kurumba* in 1938 [67], he noted that it swam at great speed, but he could not observe any method of locomotion. Finally, the creature seen three times by Mr Duncan at Bribie Island [82] had a fish-like tail, which it "flipped". And that is really all we have regarding the long necked variety. Rereading the accounts, you will also notice that, despite the long neck, the bodies of these animals were very different. I have no explanation for that. Nevertheless, it would appear that the long necked variety has a tail, which may or may not be furnished with a fluke, but that its body does not flex much while swimming. Probably it moves by means of paddles and a tail, both of which usually remain unseen.

The one creature which really does appear to be a primitive whale, perhaps a juvenile specimen, was the one which frequented

Deception Bay in 1959-60 [76]. One of the best attested sightings, it was seen at close quarters to be hairless, and to swim with vertical undulations. The fact that its nostrils were not high on its head like a modern whale's blowhole only demonstrates its primitive nature. However, its neck was relatively short, and it is uncertain where it fits into the general scheme of things.

Another sea serpent type listed by Heuvelmans was the "many humped". Particularly common off the shores of New England in the U.S.A., its body consisted of a series of humps in a "string of buoys" pattern, attached to the head with a relatively short neck. Off Australia, this might include the one off Géographe Bay in 1879 [6], the Jervis Bay creature [42], as well as [74], seen in Darwin harbour in 1980. Those three, you will note, possessed dorsal fins on the humps. In contrast, [82] had two humps, vertical undulations, and possibly a horizontal tail.

There are a few other cases reported of vertical undulations, but the presence of humps is uncertain. And what are we to make of the sea serpents sighted by the *Whangape* [21] and the *Chillagoe* [22]? The former apparently possessed a pair of pectoral fins or paddles, and undulated, but the brief description provided no details as to whether it undulated horizontally or vertically, or whether humps or coils were present. Indeed, we don't know anything about the length of the neck. For all we know, it could have been a long necked sea serpent which hadn't bothered to raise its head. The second raised its head, and had four dorsal fins. However, since the witnesses likened it to the one reported by the *Princess*, I suspect that the neck was not long, nor the body humped. It is all very mysterious.

So just what are these mysterious creatures visiting our shores? To that I can give an unequivocal answer: *I don't know*. Clearly more than one species is involved. On the balance of probabilities, I would guess the majority represent separate evolutions from the basal whale lineage. There are probably also exceptionally large eels and/or sea snakes. And, of course, I have already identified [5] as a giant salp chain.

But although we don't know what sea serpents may be, they certainly exist. Compared to better known marine species, they are rare, or at least uncommon. They are also solitary by nature; you won't find them migrating in pods or herds like the familiar humpbacked whale. Their serpentine shape allows them to wriggle out of the shallows, so they don't get stranded. (But what about [33]: the Sorrento beach stranding)? They also probably use echolocation, like whales and dolphins, and so avoid our fishing nets. In other words, a body is not going to fall into our hands any time soon, so the mystery will continue for a long time to come.

Another thing: although our population has increased five fold in the last hundred years, less than a quarter of the sightings, genuine or bogus, date from after the Second World War, and none at all from the twenty-first century. I doubt very much if all these species had suffered catastrophic population crashes in the middle of the last century. It is far more likely that people still see them, but are afraid to tell the world, and journalists are not prepared to take them seriously. So if this book encourages more witnesses to come forward, it will have served its purpose.

Appendix 1: Can You Help?

Sea serpents will not divulge their secrets readily, so feedback from the public is necessary. If you can provide any additional information, please go to my mystery animals website, https://malcolmscryptids.blogspot.com.au. At the top you can click on the button, "How to report a sighting" or, if you like, you can go straight to the page at https://malcolmscryptids.blogspot.com.au/p/how-to-report-sighting.html. This will lead you to my e-mail address, as well as a list of information required (not just on sea serpents).

As far as historical cases go, I think I have been quite successful in locating all the digitalised newspaper articles, but it is possible a couple have been missed. Those later than the early 1950s are another matter, and if anyone knows of such a report, I would be grateful for the information. I am particularly interested in the Darwin case of 1955, and the report(s) by the lighthouse keeper at Gabo Island in the 1960s.

As far as first hand testimony goes, you will probably never see a sea serpent, but if you do, your information is important. Also, as explained in Chapter 13, although I consider Rex Gilroy to be unreliable, it is not possible to rule out everything he says, and it would be useful if any genuine witnesses of his were to come forward. Also, if you are a journalist, and hear of a sighting, for goodness sake don't just restrict yourself to what the informant volunteered. Ask for more information.

Important:
The whole point of gathering information on unknown animals is to collect a corpus of information which can be examined for common features, and lead to further research, hopefully to the identification and capture of a new species. Therefore, anything you say is likely to be published. So, *if you do not want your name published, please notify me at the onset*. I will guarantee to protect your anonymity. (But if you want to remain

anonymous even to me, at least tell me whether I should describe you as a "he" or a"she".)

Nevertheless, it would be useful if you included a telephone number, and also an address if possible, in case I need to question you about some aspects of the case. These will never be included in any report.

How to report

The last thing I want is to inspire my readers to go off half-cocked. We all know what happens when you go off half cocked. You shoot yourself in the foot.

So, if you happen to see something peculiar, think! Could it have a mundane explanation? If, after your second thought, you are still convinced it cannot be explained, write down what you saw at once. If you haven't any notebook, jot down the cardinal points on a newspaper, paper towel, or whatever, until you have time to produce a full account. If you are utterly out of writing material, at least rehearse the whole event in you mind until you have time to write it. In your account, be specific. At the same time, don't be too definite. If you are uncertain about a particular feature, say so.

If you are in a group, do not discuss it among yourselves until you have put it on paper. If you do, you may well influence one another, and your testimony will lose its value.

When interviewing witnesses, let them tell their story, then ask for further information. Stress the importance of providing full details, but also to state when they are uncertain. Do not offer any suggested explanations until the interview is over. Do not ask any leading questions. (Ask misleading questions if you wish.) Ask them to draw a picture if possible, regardless of their artistic skill. When you have completed your check sheet of information, it is permissible to show pictures of animals you suspect might have been responsible. If there are multiple witnesses to the same event, make sure that they are interviewed separately, and request that they not discuss the matter with one another until it is over.

Useful Information

Please describe the event as it took place, and the animal as it appeared to you. In this regard, the following details would be useful, but not exclusive.

1. The status of the witnesses: sex, age, occupation, any special qualifications in observation or identification.

2. The date and time of the sighting, the weather and lighting conditions.

3. How long the sighting lasted.

4. The maximum and minimum distances between animal and you. Did you have any objective method of estimation?

5. The size of the animal, both height and length, with and without the tail. Again, was there any way to estimate it objectively?

6. Colour - on both upper and lower parts of body.

7. Whether the skin appeared furred, smooth, or scaly. Information like this is essential in determining to which group of animals the creature belongs.

8. The shape of the head, with the presence and position of visible eyes, ears, breathing tubes etc.

9. The length, thickness and shape of the neck. Was it clearly demarcated from the body and/or the head? Was there any mane?

10. The presence or absence of any humps, their relative size and spacing, and whether they appeared to be integral to the body shape, or merely an artefact of the body's undulations.

11. Shape of the tail, if visible. Again, do not infer its existence because of the wake. A seal would merely have a pair of flippers attached to its rear.

12. Method of propulsion: paddling, sculling, or undulating. (As a general rule, mammals undulate vertically, other life forms horizontally.)

13. Method of surfacing and submerging. (Most animals will dive, but certain types of sea serpent simply sink like a stone.)

14. Any other behaviour not otherwise recorded.

15. Names and addresses of anyone else who may have had a similar experience.

16. Anything else you might consider relevant.

If you have the presence of mind to record all that, you will be rewarded with a memory that will stick in your mind forever. You will also deserve a medal. More to the point, if you are interviewing someone, at least ask those questions. They might end up remembering more than they originally volunteered.

Appendix 2: Maps

For **Map 1**: Northern Territory Coast (Top End), see page 101.

For **Map 2**: Moreton Bay, Queensland, see page 102.

Map 3: Queensland North of Tropic of Capricorn

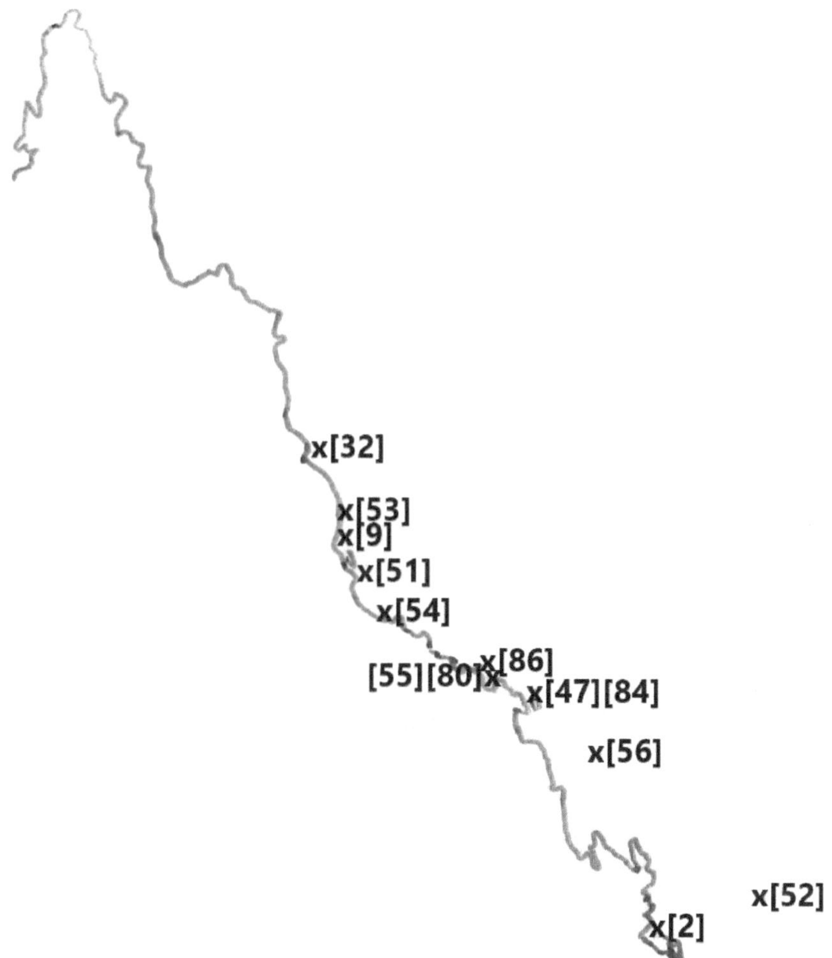

Map 4: Queensland South of Tropic of Capricorn

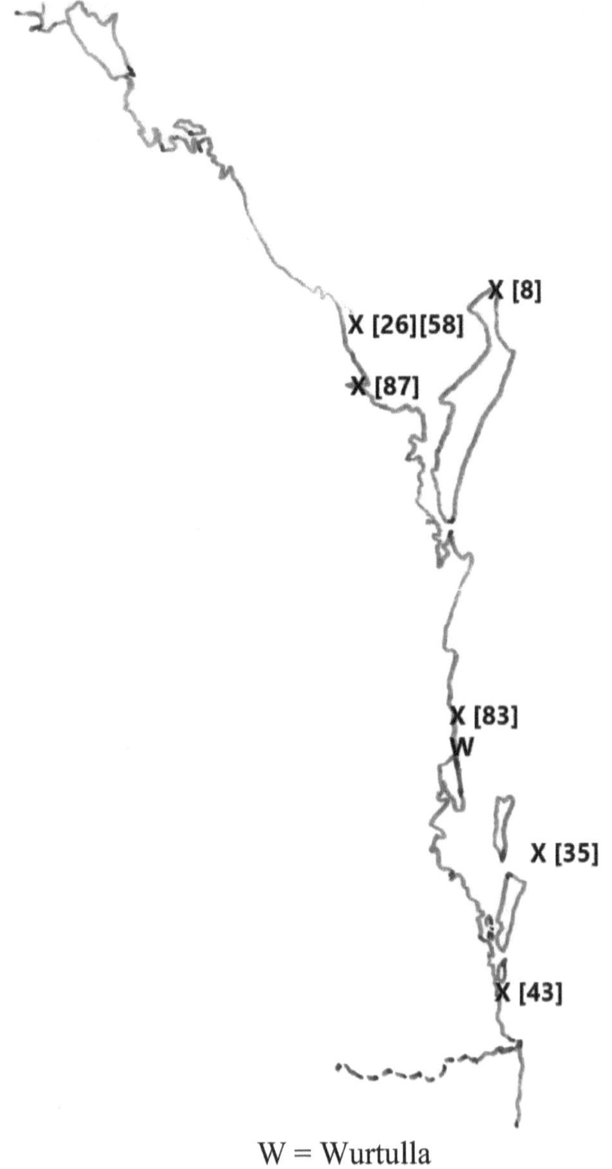

W = Wurtulla

See Map 2 (p 102 for details of southernmost section (Moreton Bay)

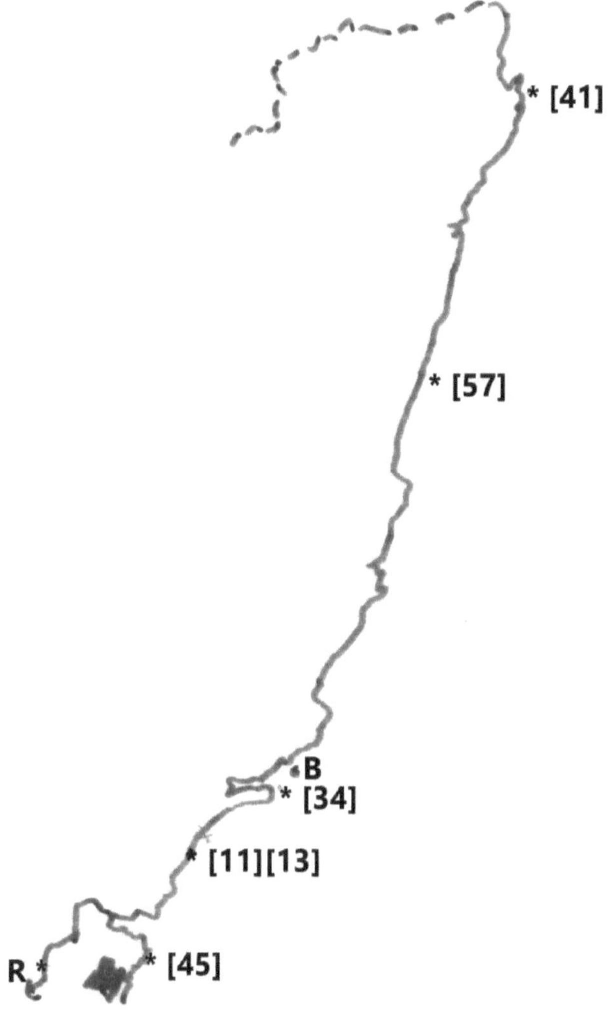

Map 5: New South Wales north of Sydney

B = Broughton Island
R = approximate location of Rousek's sighting

Map 6: New South Wales south of Sydney

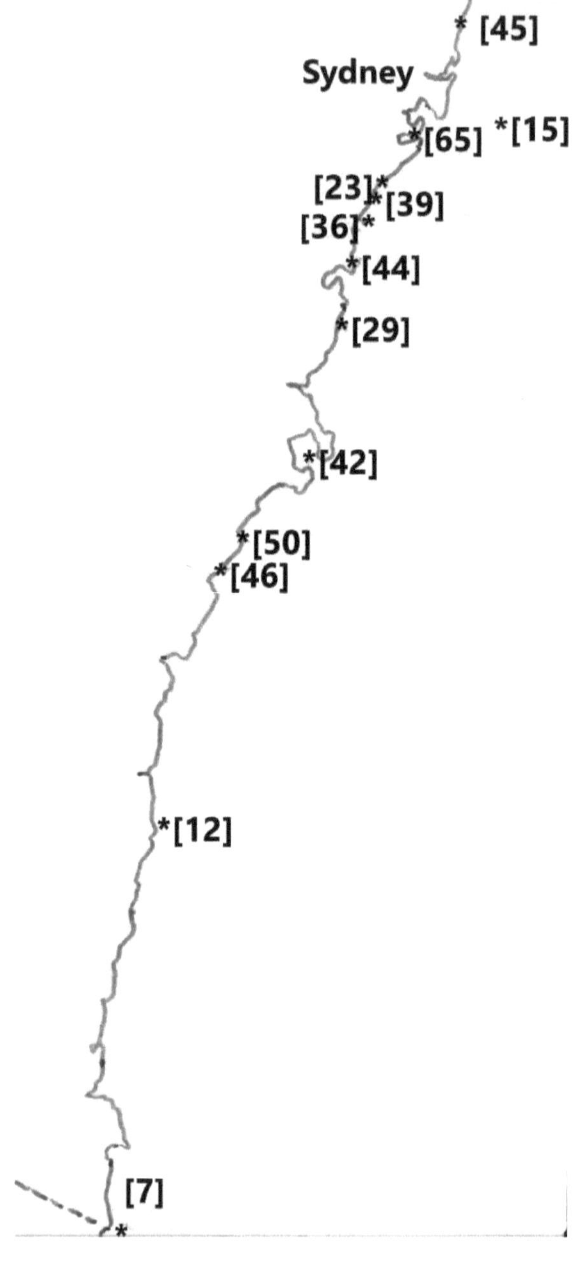

Map 7: Victoria (exclusive of Port Phillip area)

G = Gabo Island

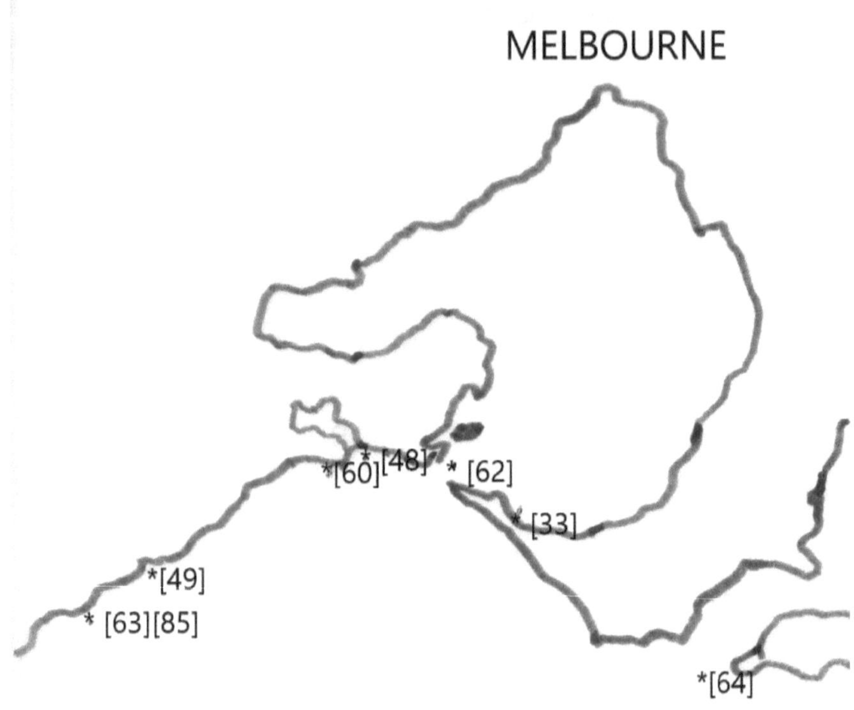

Map 8: Port Phillip Bay area, Victoria

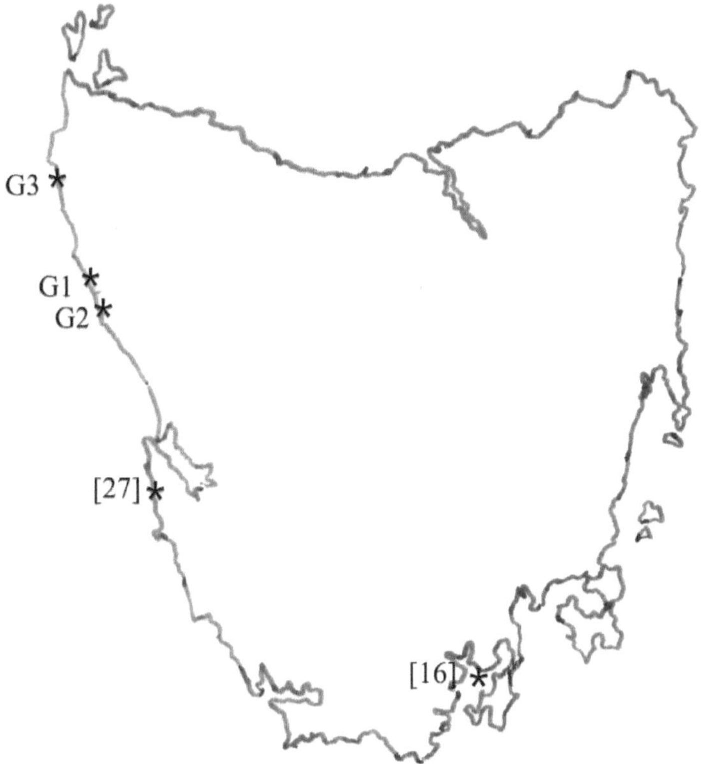

G1, G2, G3 = Approximate positions of the globsters of 1962, 1970, and 1998 respectively

Map 10: South Australia

Map 11: South west Western Australia

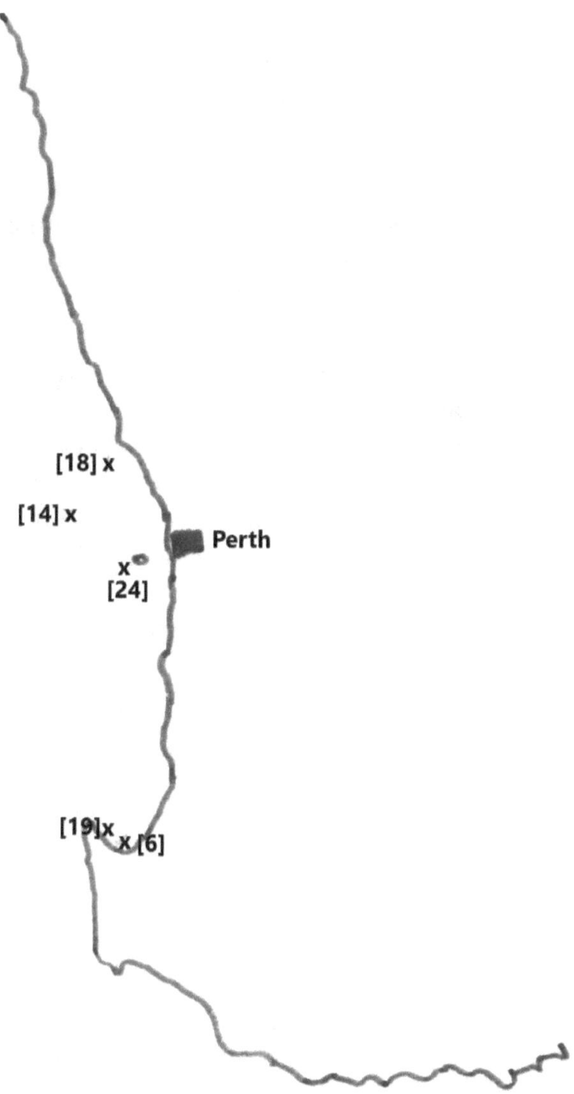

Note: [24] is also the approximate position of "Herbert's" encounter

References

Introduction

[1] English translation, with additions: Bernard Heuvelmans (1968), *In the Wake of the Sea-Serpents* (Rupert Hart-Davis)
[2] http://trove.nla.gov.au

Chapter 1
[3] Roesch, Ben S. (1998). A critical evaluation of the supposed contemporary existence of *Carcharodon megalodon. The Cryptozoology Review* 3(2): 14-24, also online as http://web.ncf.ca/bz050/megalodon   accessed 22.6.18
[4] Stead, David G. (1963). *Sharks and Rays of Australian Seas.* London, Angus and Robertson, pp 45-46.
[5] ' "White Death" Startling Shark Story. Is It 115 Feet Long? Mystery at Port Stephens', *The Sun* (Sydney) Wed 30 Jan 1918, page 5, 'Very Like a Whale. Shark That Eats Lobster Pots. Queer Story from Port Stephens', *Evening News* (Sydney) Wed 30 Jan 1918, page 4
[6] Wood, Gerald L. (1972), *The Guinness Book of Animal Facts and Feats*, first edition, p 221,
[7] I published the details of these interviews on http://malcolmscryptids.blogspot.com.au/2012/07/what-was-that-big-fish.html

Chapter 2
[8] *The Banner* (Melbourne), Friday 17 March 1854, page 10. This was a short-lived, biweekly newspaper. Captain Aschlund originally released the story to the *Bode,* which I presume was a Dutch East Indies newspaper, and it was then picked up by the *Straits Times Express* of Singapore.
[9] 'An Australian Sea Serpent', *Evening News* (Sydney), Fri 6 December 1889, p 5
[10] See Robert Nicholson (1965), *The Pitcairners*, Angus and Robertson, republished in paperback by Pasifika Press, Auckland, 1997. Also: Richard Hough (1972), *Captain Bligh and Mr. Christian. The men and the mutiny*, Hutchinson

[11] Letter to Captain G. Drevar, 1883: cited by Heuvelmans (ref **1**), pp 251 and 605.

[12] Adams, John (1877), Account of a supposed sea-serpent seen off Nepean Island, *Proc. Lit. Phil. Soc. Lpool*, London and Liverpool, no. 31, p 68, cited in Heuvelmans (ref **1**), pp 250-251.

[13] Cited by Heuvelmans (ref 1) p 283

[14] For example, 'Sea Serpent off the Coast', *The Evening News* (Sydney), Tues 4 Dec 1877, p 2.

[15] For example, *The Toowoomba Chronicle and Darling Downs General Advertiser* (Queensland) and *The South Australian Register* (Adelaide), both of 4 Dec 1877.

[16] Roy P. Mackal (1980), *Searching for Hidden Animals*, Doubleday Books

[17] Hamish Robertson, '*Pyrostremma spinosum* (Giant fire salp)' http://www.biodiversityexplorer.org/mm/tunicates/pyrostremma_s pinosum.htm (accessed 22.1.18)

[18] *South Australian Register* (Adelaide), Mon. 7 April 1879, page 5

[19] Barnett, H.C. (1879), 'The Sea-Serpent', *Nature*, London, 24 July 1879, pp 289-290

[20] *Wallaroo Times and Mining Journal* (Port Wallaroo, SA), Wed. 13 Aug 1879, page 2

Chapter 3

[21] Biographic data summarised by Ulrich Magin (2014), New material on the moha-moha, *J. Cryptozoology* 3:21-31, who cited Williams, F. (2002), *Princess K'Gari's Fraser Island: A History of Fraser Island*, self published.

[22] I have been unable to access this journal, and am relying on the quotations from R. T. Gould (1930), *The Case for the Sea-Serpent*, Philip Allan, chapter 7.

[23] Williams, cited by Magin. See reference 21 above.

[24] Saville-Kent, W. (c 1893), *The Great Barrier Reef of Australia*, pp 323 - 26.

[25] If anyone is interested, I published a layman's guide to scientific names on line at

https://malcolmsmiscellany.blogspot.com.au/2015/09/understanding-those-strange-scientific.html

26 Gould (ref. 20) p 181

27 Magin (ref. 19) p 23

28 Heuvelmans (ref 1) p 301

29 Magin, Ulrich (2014), , New material on the moha-moha, *J. Cryptozoology* 3:21-31. See also my critique of the paper in http://malcolmscryptids.blogspot.com.au/2015/06/journal-of-cryptozoology-volume-3.html

Chapter 4

30 'The Fabled Monster. The Sea Serpent Sighted', *The Australian Star* (Sydney) Tues 3 June 1890, page 7

'A Sea Serpent. The Monster in Full View', *Singleton Argus* (NSW) Wed 4 June 1890, page 4, and others with slightly different wording.

31 I have taken this summary from Gould, R. T. (1930), *The Case for the Sea-Serpent*, Philip Allan, London, pp 254-5, and 'The Bishop and the Sea Serpent' *Border Watch* (Mt. Gambier, SA) Wed 27 Jan 1892, p 4, and other newspapers.

32 Oudemans, Antoon C. (1892), *The Great Sea Serpent*, self published. This book can be read or downloaded at https://archive.org/details/greatseaserpenth00oude (accessed 12.2.17)

33 'Sea Monster in the Harbour. Escape of a Diver', *Newcastle Morning Herald and Miners' Advocate* (NSW) Wed 18 Nov 1891, p 8

34 'Another Sea Monster in the Harbour. Captured and on Exhibition', *ibid.* Mon 7 Dec 1891, p 5

35 'The Sea Monster's Mate Captured. Together in Life and Death', *ibid.* Tues 8 Dec 1891.

36 'The Sea Serpent Again', *The Age* (Melbourne), Mon. 3 April 1893, page 6

37 'A Sea Serpent. Seen at Newcastle. Conflict with a Whale', *Evening News* (Sydney) Mon. 27 August 1894, page 6, and multiple later newspapers.

[38] 'The Sea Serpent Again', *Newcastle Morning Herald and Miners' Advocate,* Wed 14 Oct 1896, page 5

[39] 'A message from the Sea', *South Eastern Times* (Millicent, SA), Fri. 7 Jan 1910, page 2

[40] Wikipedia, citing *Ships of the Royal Navy* by J. J. Colledge

[41] 'The Sea Serpent Again', *Daily Telegraph* (Sydney), Wed 30 June 1897, page 5

[42] ' A Sea Serpent. Chases a Fisherman,' *The Mercury* (Hobart) Thurs 3 August 1899, page 3

[43] 'The Sea Serpent Again', *Daily Telegraph* (Sydney), Thurs 10 Aug 1899, page 5

Chapter 5

[44] 'The Sea Serpent Again', *Gouldburn Evening Penny Post*, Thurday 16 August 1900, page 2

[45] 'About the Sea Serpent. A Man Who Has Seen It', *South Australian Register*, Thurs 30 August 1900, page 3

[46] 'The Sea Serpent. Two Hundred Feet Long', *Coolgardie Miner* (W.A.) Fri 12 Oct 1900, page 6.

[47] Laurence Thomson (1901), 'How we saw the "Sea Serpent"', *Wide World Magazine* vol. 6: 566-9. This can be read or downloaded at https://archive.org/details/wideworldmagazin06londuoft (accessed 19.2.18). I also copied the text at http://malcolmscryptids.blogspot.com.au/2015/12/the-nemesis-sea-serpent-of-1900.html .

[48] 'Attacked by a Sea Monster', *The Age* (Melbourne), Thurs 16 May 1901, page 6

[49] 'The Sea Serpent', *Otago Daily Times*, 25 July 1902, page 5, and *Timaru Herald*, same date, page 3

[50] 'A Glimpse of a Sea Monster', *Sydney Morning Herald*, Mon 14 July 1902, page 8

[51] 'Clifton', *South Coast Times and Wollongong Argus*, Sat 16 April 1904, page 11

[52] 'Mysterious Fish. The Yongala's Experience', *West Australian* (Perth), Fri 29 July 1904, page 3

[53] 'Sea Serpent Again', *Daily Telegraph* (Sydney), Sat 25 January 1908, page 8

[54] 'A Sea Serpent', *Bundaberg Mail and Burnett Advertiser*, Wed. 13 October 1909, page 2

[55] 'Alleged Sea Serpent at Elliott Heads', *ibid* Mon. 18 October 1909, page 2

[56] 'Is It a Sea Serpent? A West Coast Discovery', *The North Western Advocate and the Emu Bay Times* (Tas.), Mon 26 May 1913, page 3.

[57] 'A Strange Animal. Discovery in the North-West', *The Examiner* (Launceston, Tas.) Sat 24 May 1913, page 9

[58] I have drawn predominantly from the following: 'The Sea Serpent. Seen Off Australian Coast. Described by Dimboola's Captain', *Sun* (Sydney) Tues 20 May 1913, page 6 (initial report); 'A Strange Sea Monster', *Sunday Times* (Perth), Sun 25 May 1913, page 14 (captain's written statement and sketch); and 'The Sad-Eyed Sea Serpent', *Daily Telegraph* (Sydney), Sat 31 May 1913, page 15 (another interview and another sketch)

[59] 'Captain Sees the Joke', Melbourne *Herald*, Thurs 29 May 1913, page 8

[60] 'Sea Serpent. Sceptical Expert. Mr. Dannevig's Views', Melbourne *Herald,* Wed 21 May 1913, page 7

[61] '"Sea Serpent". Strange Sight Witnessed. Shoal of Seals', Melbourne *Herald*, Fri 20 June 1913, page 9

[62] 'Did the Dimboola Captain See a Cuttle-fish with Arms 30 ft. or More in Length?' *The Daily Telegraph* (Sydney), Thurs 22 May 1913, page 11

[63] Richard Ellis (1998), *In search of the giant squid*, The Lyons Press, also Penguin, 1999.

[64] See my articles at
http://malcolmscryptids.blogspot.com.au/2016/10/really-gigantic-squid-1-official-records.html and
http://malcolmscryptids.blogspot.com.au/2016/10/really-gigantic-squid-2-big-ones-that.html

Chapter 6
[65] 'A Sea Serpent', *The Richmond River Express and Casino Kyogle Advertiser* (NSW), Fri 21 Feb. 1991, page 2. The original apparently came from the *Kiama Reporter*, but I have been unable to access it.
[66] 'He Saw a Serpent', *Richmond River Herald and Northern Districts Advertiser* (NSW), Tues 8 April 1919, page 2
[67] 'Seen At Beachport. A Strange Sea Monster', *Express and Telegraph* (Adelaide), Thurs 22 April 1920, page 2
[68] 'Was it a Sea-Serpent. To the Editor,' Melbourne *Herald*, Thurs 17 November 1921, page 13
[69] 'Sea Serpents Do Exist!', *Daily Pictorial* (Sydney), 16 June 1930
[70] 'Saw Sea-Serpent at Sorrento. 30 ft Long, Thick as Motor Tyre', *The Herald* (Melbourne) Sat 19 Jan 1929, page 6
[71] 'Sea Serpent', *Northern Champion* (Taree, NSW), Wed 11 Feb 1925, page 2
[72] Chevey, P. (1937), 'Observation inédite sur un animal marin de grande taille observé sur la côte de l'Australie, en 1925', *Bull. Soc. Zool. Fr.*, Paris, no. 62, cited by Heuvelmans (ref. **i**) p 427
[73] de Haan, P. 'Een Zeeslang?' *De Zee* (Den Helder) 48 (23.7.1925), cited by Heuvelmans (ref. **i**) pp 410-411. Heuvelmans also kindly provided me with a French translation.
[74] 'Sea Serpent Seen Off Bellambi Shore', *Sunday Times* (Sydney) Sun. 15 August 1926, page 1
[75] Letter to John Scott Hughes, 6 Dec 1953, in the possession of Mrs Lilian Rawlings, cited by Heuvelmans (ref. **i**), page 432.

Chapter 7
[76] 'A Sea Serpent', *South Coast Times and Wollongong Argus*, Fri. 13 June 1930, page 21,
'Bellambi Fishermen Report Seeing Sea Serpent', *Barrier Miner* (Broken Hill), Fri. 13 June 1930, page 4,
'Ocean Monster's Roar', *Evening News* (Sydney), Sat. 14 June 1930, page 2.

77 '"It's Real" That Sea Serpent. S. Coast Knows It', *Sun* (Sydney) Fri 13 June 1930, page 10

78 'A Whale? Sea Serpent Story. Expert View', *The Sun* (Sydney) Sun 15 June 1930, page 5

79 'Fearsome Monster at Sea Seen From Cliffs', *The Sun* (Sydney) Thurs 3 July 1930, page 17

80 'Sea Serpent Seen Again. "Frightful looking: 80 or 90 feet long"', *The Register News-Pictorial* (Adelaide), Thurs 3 July 1930, page 3

81 '"No Doubt" That Sea Serpent More See It', *The Sun* (Sydney) Sat 5 July 1930, page 3

82 'Good View of Sea Serpent', *Evening News* (Sydney), Sat 5 July 1930, page 5

83 'Barnacled Log "Sea Serpent"', *Casino and Kyogle Courier and North Coast Advertiser* (NSW), Wed 16 July 1930, page 3

84 'Saw Sea Serpent. Saucer Eyes', *Manning River Times and Advocate for the Northern Coasts Districts of New South Wales* (Taree), Sat 12 July 1930, page 7

85 'Monster of the Deep. Incident Near Cape Byron', *Telegraph* (Brisbane), Sat 26 July 1930, page 5

86 'The Sea Serpent. Fisheries Expert's Opinion', *Singleton Argus* (NSW), Wed 6 Aug 1930, page 3

87 'Has Sea Serpent Returned to Jervis Bay? Sydney businessmen claim to have seen it.' *Evening News* (Rockhampton, Qld), Fri 8 Aug 1930, page 7

88 '"Sea Serpent" Again. Monster Off South Coast'. *The Telegraph* (Brisbane), Mon 4 Aug 1930, page 8

89 '"It's Real" That Sea Serpent. S. Coast Knows It', *Sun* (Sydney) Fri 13 June 1930, page 10

90 'Stockton's "Sea Serpent"', *Newcastle Morning Herald and Miners' Advocate*, Sat. 9 Aug 1930, page 8

91 'Curious Creature. Sea Serpent at Southport?' *Queensland Times* (Ipswich), Mon. 11 Aug 1930, page 7

92 '100ft. Sea Serpent!' *Kyogle Examiner* (N.S.W.) Fri 12 Sept 1930, page 3

⁹³ 'Like Mast. Sea Snake's Tail. Four Saw It', *Sun* (Sydney) Tues 18 Nov 1930, page 16
⁹⁴ 'Fisherman's Story. South Coast "Sea Serpent"', *Sydney Morning Herald*, Wed 4 Feb 1931, page 4
⁹⁵ "Sea Serpent", *Mudgee Guardian and North-Western Representative* (NSW) Mon 20 July 1931, page 5
⁹⁶ 'Sea Leopard Captured. Now in Aquarium.' *Northern Miner* (Charters Towers, Qld), Mon 3 Aug 1931, page 4
⁹⁷ Norman Caldwell, in collaboration with Norman Ellison (1936), *Fangs of the Sea*, Angus and Robertson. The first instance was described on pp 113-114 of the 1937 edition, and the second on pp 112-113 of the 1966 edition.

Chapter 8
⁹⁸ I copied most of the original reports on http://malcolmscryptids.blogspot.com.au/2014/02/the-year-of-sea-serpents-1934.html
⁹⁹ 'Another Sea Serpent. At Victoria Resort', *The Courier-Mail* (Brisbane), Fri 1st Feb 1934, page 12
¹⁰⁰ 'Strange Sea Monster. Victorian Fishermen's Experience', *The Courier-Mail* (Brisbane), Thurs 22 Feb 1934, page 13
¹⁰¹ 'Sea Serpent?', *The Shoalhaven News and South Coast Districts Advertiser*, Sat 10 March 1934, page 2.
¹⁰² '"Shooting" Films Among Sharks', *The Courier-Mail* (Brisbane), Sat 4 Aug 1934, page 17
¹⁰³ 'Northern Sea Monster. Eye Witness's Description', *Telegraph* (Brisbane), Tues 14 Aug 1934, page 8
¹⁰⁴ 'Monster of the Deep. Seen by Fishermen When Trailing Off Barrier Reef',*Townsville Daily Bulletin*, Thurs 4 Oct 1934, page 7
¹⁰⁵ '"Loch Ness Monster" at Mourilyan? Launch Party Tells of "Sea Serpent"', *The Courier-Mail* (Brisbane), Tues 14 Aug 1934, page 13.
¹⁰⁶ 'Monster of the Sea. Seen in Cleveland Bay. Head Like Huge Turtle', *Townsville Daily Bulletin*, Mon 20 Aug 1934, page 5

Mattingley, A. H. E. (Aug 1935), 'The Sea-Serpent? Strange Marine Creature Observed off Coast of Queensland', *Vict. Nat. 52: 74-5*

[107] 'The Sea Monster. Seen Three Times on Sunday', *Townsville Daily Bulletin*, Tues 21 Aug 1934, page 5

[108] 'Sea Serpent Again. Sighted by Bowen Fishermen', *Telegraph* (Brisbane), Fri 24 Aug 1934, page 3

[109] 'Sighted Again. Mariner's Wireless Report', *Townsville Daily Bulletin*, Sat 1st Sept 1934, page 7

[110] 'Sea Creature Reported by Fishermen. 40 Feet in Length'. *Sydney Morning Herald*, Fri 14 Sept 1934, page 11

[111] 'Sea Serpent? Seen Near Burnett River', *Telegraph* (Brisbane), Thurs 11 Oct 1934, page 19

[112] 'The Loch Ness Monster. Appearance at Portland.' *Portland Guardian*, Mon 24 June 1935, page 2

[113] 'Strange Sea Creature. Workmen Attempt to Lasso It. Had Coat of Fur', *News* (Adelaide), Tues 30 July 1935, front page

[114] '"Sea Serpent". Eyes Like Saucers. Has Many Characteristics. Barwon Heads Mystery', *Morning Bulletin* (Rockhampton, Qld), Wed 31 July 1935, page 7

[115] 'Like Saucers. "Sea Serpent's" Eyes', *The Sun* (Sydney), Tues 30 July 1935, page 11

[116] His story can be found in the two comments by 'Anonymous' of 18 March 2018, on my blog post of http://malcolmscryptids.blogspot.com.au/2017/08/anitpodean-sea-serpents-1932-9.html .

[117] 'Report of Sea Serpent Draws Crowd of Searchers. Independent Sketches Are Identical', *News* (Adelaide), Wed 31 July 1935, page 1

[118] 'Weird Monsters. Two from Victoria', *The Central Queensland Herald* (Rockhampton), Thurs 8 Aug 1935, page 49

[119] 'Sea Serpent Reappears: "Like Toothed Whale"', *Mail* (Adelaide), Sat 3 Aug 1935, page 2

[120] 'Sea Serpent. Seen at Cronulla', *Manilla Express* (NSW) Tues 10 Dec 1935, page 4

121 I copied the relevant Australian news articles in my blog at
http://malcolmscryptids.blogspot.com.au/2017/08/anitpodean-sea-s
erpents-1932-9.html

Chapter 9
122 Captain T.W. Arthur, 'Sea Serpents. And Other Monsters.',
Sydney Morning Herald, Sat 28 April 1934, page 10
123 (ex-Leading Seaman) C. W. Walters, 'Sea Monster?', *The
Sun-Herald* Sydney) 30 November 1980
124 Full details in: Paul Cropper and Malcolm Smith (1992),
Some unpublicized Australasian "sea serpent" reports.
Cryptozoology 11: 51 - 69
125 ' "Monster" reported in Darwin Harbour', *The Canberra Times*,
Thurs. 12 May 1955, page 1
126 'Is a sea 'thing' lurking in harbor?' *The Northern Territory
News*. Tues 13 October 1959, page 1
127 'Is that friendly ray the great Mandorah Monster?'   *ibid*. Fri.
16 October 1959
128 'Mandorah Monster nearly ended it's career on beach', *ibid*.
Tues. 20 Oct 1959
129 'Security and the monster', *ibid*. Fri 23 October 1959
130 'Monster 'not fish' - Carter', *ibid*. Fri. 6 November 1959
131 Peter Cain, 'Is this Mandorah's Loch Ness.', *Northern
Territorian*. Sat 14 April 2001, p15
132 'Monster at Maningrida?', *Maningrida Mirage* vol. 142 (23
June 1972)
133 'Dinosaur found in NT Harbor', *The Northern Territory News*,
Sat. 2 February 1980, page 1.
See also 'Darwin dinosaur creates puzzle', *Sunday Times* (Perth)
10 February 1980
134 Fred McCue, 'More to monsters than meet the eye', *The
Northern Territory News,* Fri 15 February 1980
135 Fred McCue, 'Five see mystery object', *ibid.* Wednesday 20
February 1980, page 1

Chapter 10

[136] I have published all the documents in full online at http://malcolmscryptids.blogspot.com.au/2014/05/the-original-deception-bay-monsters.html

[137] 'Sea 'horror' at Toorbul,' *Courier-Mail* (Brisbane) Sat 27 November 1948, page 1

[138] ''Serpent' Catch: Now Believed Sea Snake', *ibid.* Tues 14 December 1948, page 1

[139] 'Toorbul "monster". Now It's a Turtle', *ibid.* Mon 29 November 1948, page 3

[140] 'Loch Ness Monster in Our Bay', *Truth* (Brisbane), Sun 3 Jan 1960

[141] 'Search for Bay Creature', clipping from unidentified newspaper, but probably the *Telegraph* (Brisbane) of 2 January 1960.

[142] 'They Saw the Monster', *Truth* (Brisbane), Sunday 10 January 1960

[143] 'Here's Our Monster in-Chief', *ibid.* Sunday 16 October 1960.

[144] For this calculation, I used http://www.thomblake.com.au/secondary/hisdata/calculate.php

[145] *Truth* (Brisbane), Sun 16 October 1960, page 2

[146] *ibid.* Sun 9 October 1960, page 2

[147] *ibid.* Sun 2 October 1960, page 2

[148] ''Monster' seen off Bribie Island', *Courier-Mail* (Brisbane), Wed 26 Sept 1962

[149] 'That monster came again', clipping from unidentified Brisbane newspaper dated Tues 9 Oct 1962. I suspect it was the Brisbane evening paper, the *Telegraph*, but I have been unable to find it. It was published by the same company as the *Courier-Mail*, but it also run to two editions, the "City Final" and "Late Extra". They were 99% the same, but not 100%, and reference libraries seldom carry both editions.

[150] 'The Thing' bobs up again North', *Australasian Post*, 6 December 1962

Chapter 11

[151] I have abstracted this story from the front page accounts in the *The Mercury* (Hobart) of 8 to 19 March 1962, and to the article, 'Bermuda blog remains unidentified,' *The ISC Newsletter* 7(3): 1-6 (Autumn, 1988). This was the newsletter of the now defunct International Society of Cryptozoology.

[152] ''Monster' may be big find.' *The Mercury* (Hobart), Thurs 8 March 1962, page 1

[153] '"Sea Monster" Find May Become World Topic' *ibid.* Fri 9 March 1962, pp 1,2

[154] '"Sea Monster" may be giant devil ray', *ibid.* Sat 10 March 1962, page 1

[155] "Sea Monster" may be biggest ray ever known', *ibid.* Mon 12 March 1962, page 1

[156] 'Identical to 1934 W.A. find?' *ibid.* Mon 12 March 1962, page 1

[157] 'C. S. I. R. O. experts will examine "monster"', *ibid.* Wed 14 March 1962, page 1
'Helicopter files scientists to "monster"', *ibid.* Fri. 16 March 1962, page 3
'Official silence on mystery of "monster"', *ibid.* Sat 17 March 1962, page 1

[158] ''Monster' to get thorough check', *ibid.* Mon. 19 March 1962, pages 1,2

[159] Kerry Pink, 'Unidentified "object" on beach', *The Advocate* (Burnie, Tas.) Thurs 12 Nove 1970, pages 1,2
Kerry Pink, 'That 'monster' is it a whale?' *ibid.* Fri 13 Nov 1970, pages 1,2

[160] Tim Dinsdale (1966), *The Leviathans*, Routledge & Kegan Paul, revised edition 1976 by Futura Publications, pp 163-4, citing the *Townsville Bulletin* of Wed 24 March 1965.

[161] Pierce, Sidney K. Steven E. Massey, Nicholas E. Curtis, Gerald N. Smith Jr., Carlos Olavarría, and Timothy K. Maugel (2004),

'Microscopic, biochemical, and molecular characteristics of the Chilean Blob and a comparison with the remains of other sea monsters: nothing but whales', *The Biological Bulletin* 206: 125-133
[162] ''Sea monster' mystery solved', *The Examiner* (Launceston), Thurs 8 Jan 1998, pages 1, 2

Chapter 12
[163] 'Here's That Sea Serpent Again - With Red Beard', *Sunday Mail* (Brisbane), Sun 9 Nov 1941, page 7
[164] Robert le Serrec, 'The Barrier Reef Monster', *Everybody's*, 31 March 1965, pp 8-10 (*Everybody's* was an Australian weekly magazine resulting from the amalgamation of two failing weekly, the *Australian Woman's Mirror* and *Weekend* in 1961, which lasted only till 1968.)
[165] Heuvelmans (ref.i) pp 531-5
[166] Naish, Darren, 'The amazing Hook Island sea monster photos' http://scienceblogs.com/tetrapodzoology/2008/07/07/hook-island-monster-tadpole/ (assessed 16.6.18)
[167] In addition to the witnesses' written statements to me, the most detailed contemporary accounts were:
'Has Aireys Its Own Loch Ness?' *Geelong Advertiser*, Mon 4 June 1973,
'Monster in Focus', *ibid.* Tues 5 June 1973, and
Jeff Wells, 'What Was the Thing That Rose From the Ocean?' *Melbourne Truth*, Sat 16 June 1973

Chapter 13
[168] His website, for what it is worth, is http://www.mysteriousaustralia.com (accessed 18.6.18)
[169] I covered the yowie in a chapter of *Bunyips and Bigfoots*, but the best reference work on the subject is *The Yowie, in search of Australia's bigfoot* by Tony Healy and Paul Cropper (2006), Strange Nation, Sydney
[170] Rex Gilroy (1995), *Mysterious Australia*, Nexus Publishing

¹⁷¹ Max Suich, 'The great encourager', *The Australian*, Wed. 2 June 2010   on-line at
https://www.theaustralian.com.au/arts/books/the-great-encourager/news-story/4d2188d2adc30c4d4e4f9fac256a0bb1?sv=e2943cc3077aa2670c242c4613c92213 (accessed 21.6.18)
¹⁷² 'small towns … Big Legends' *The Australian Good Taste Magazine,* January 2000
¹⁷³ 'Hideous giants inhabit Papuan seas', *The ABC Weekly*, 31 July 1943, page 26
¹⁷⁴ James Griffin, 'Henri Stanislas Verjus (1860 -1892)', *Australian Dictionary of Biography*, vol. 6 (1976) and at
http://adb.anu.edu.au/biography/verjus-henri-stanislas-4777 (accessed 21.6.18)
¹⁷⁵ Paul Cropper and Malcolm Smith (1992). Some unpublicized Australasian "sea serpent" reports.   *Cryptozoology* 11: 51 - 69

Chapter 14
¹⁷⁶ These cases can be found at
http://malcolmscryptids.blogspot.com.au/2013/06/the-trouble-with-eye-witnesses.html

.

People

Miscellaneous

Other Books by the Author

The following books are all in print, and available from Amazon.

Bunyips and Bigfoots. up-dated second edition. The classic survey of Australia's mystery animals: bunyips, sea serpents, the North Queensland tiger, Tasmanian tigers on the mainland, pumas and black panthers, yowies, and others - all fully documented. Originally published in 1996, it was republished and up-dated in 2021.

The Truth About Bunyips. Every Australian has heard about bunyips, but no-one knows what they are supposed to look like. Based on a huge number of recently digitalised old documents and newspapers, this short book should be the definitive work on the subject.

Forgotten Sea Serpents. This is an adjunct to the above: a large collection of reports of sea serpents outside of Australia which have, apparently, been missed by other researchers. The book should be welcomed by cryptozoologists looking to complete their documentation on the subject.

Forgotten Bigfoots Around the World. Here I present a series of articles - mostly my own translations - of reports from difficult-to-access journals about bigfoot type animals from the Caucasus, the Himalayan region of Pakistan, as well as Latin America, Africa, and even Europe.

Trials of a Tourist. I've been an international tourist for most of my adult life, visiting remote places even millionaires haven't seen. So now I have written a humorous account of the quirky things I have experienced, as well as the "plot against tourists", by which the world conspires to make travelling as inconvenient as possible.

Apparitions: tulpas, ghosts, fairies, and even stranger things. This is not an ordinary book on ghosts, but coves a whole range of paranormal apparitions: tulpas and other creations of the mind, ghosts, fairies, and things which are more bizarre - but all fully documented.

The Stranger from the Stars. A science fiction novel about a group of hikers who rescue an injured alien from a crashed flying saucer. Having followed the UFO scene for more than 50 years, I have ensured that the story is "realistic", in that all the phenomena described have been reported many times in the literature.

Savages and Saints by Leon and Theophila Philippi - but ghost written by yours truly. This is the story of my parents-in-law: a farm boy from Nebraska, and a pastor's daughter from the Eyre Peninsula of South Australia, who were thrown together under unusual circumstances, married after a whirlwind courtship, and set out for New Guinea as missionaries. The sort of experiences they went through are beyond the imagination of the present generation.

The Gospels: Harmonized and Annotated (two volumes): Here I present the four gospels together in chronological order, with parallel texts side by side, and with a discussion of the situation in first century Israel in which they were embedded.

A Zoologist Looks at Science Fiction. H. G. Wells said that the essence of science fiction was the suspension of disbelief. As a zoologist, I have a bit more difficulty than most. In this short book I examine the mistakes made by science fiction writers in their creations of monsters and aliens, not to mention robots.

The Repat Racket. An insider's report on Veterans' Affairs. Originally published in 2010, and now republished, it reveals the way in which good intentions for compensating ex-servicemen resulted in a grotesque legal system open to enormous abuses.